MOONCOP

MOONCOP

TOM GAULD

DRAWN & QUARTERLY

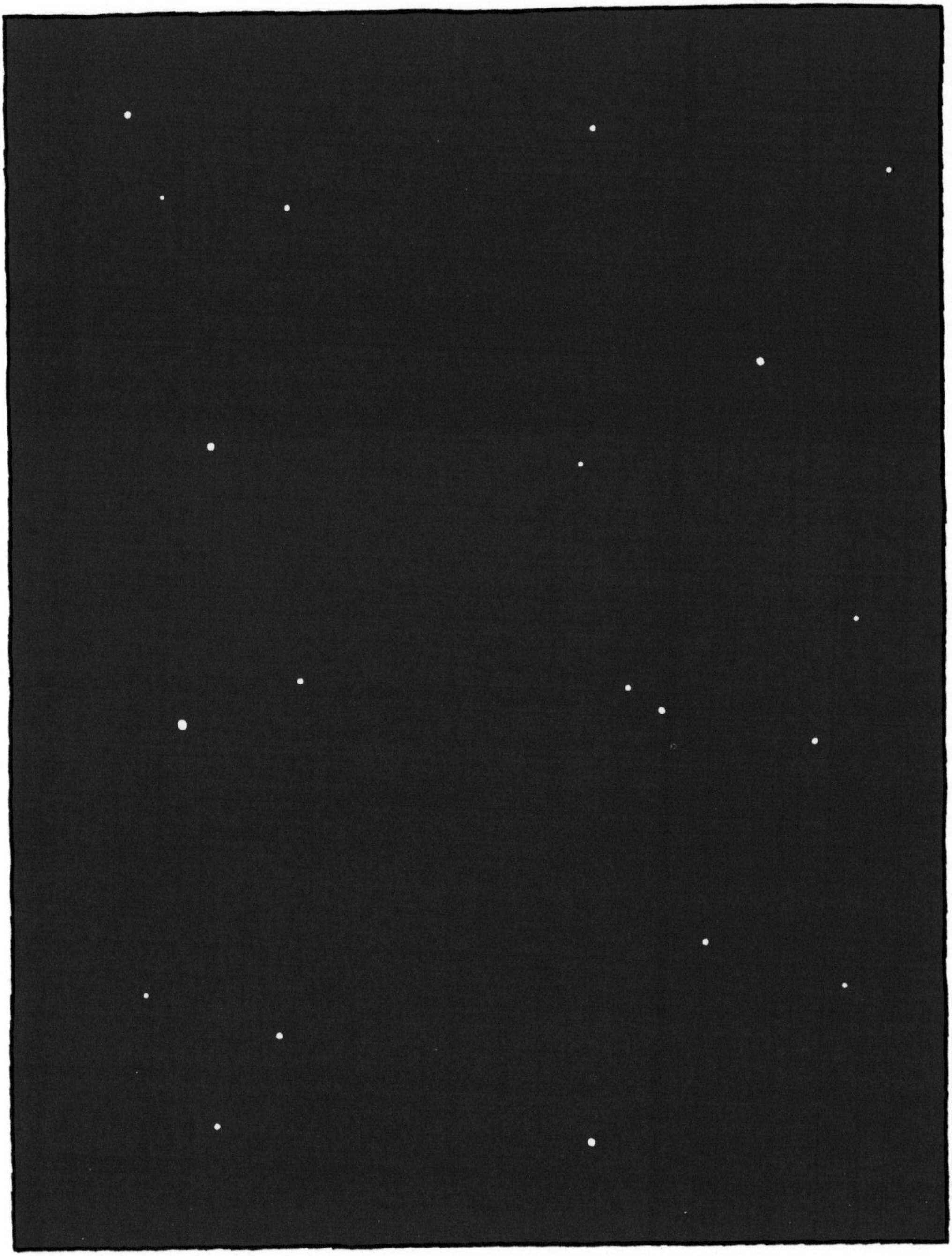

4

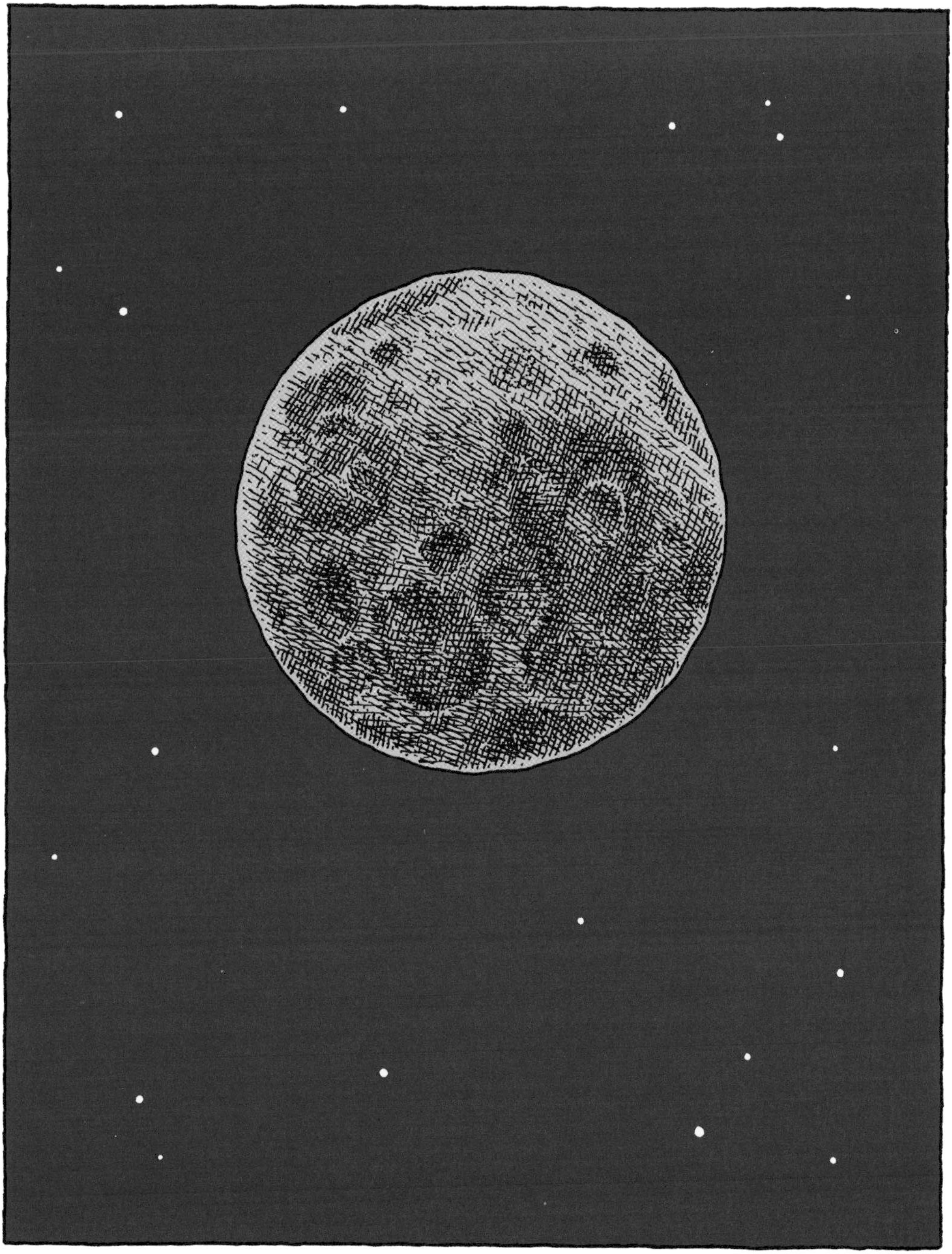

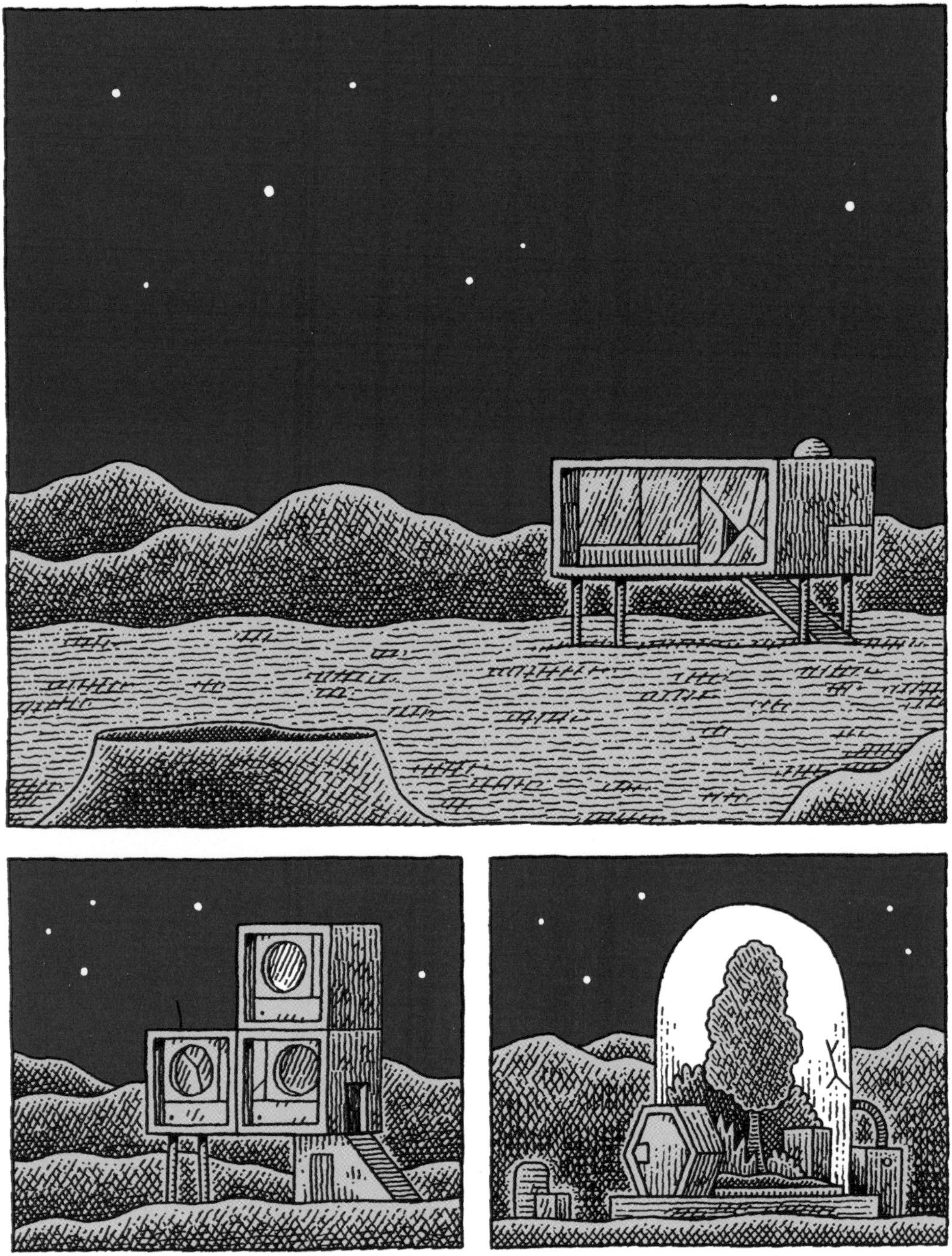

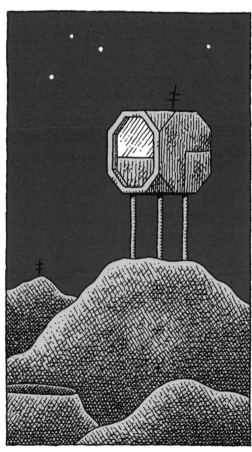

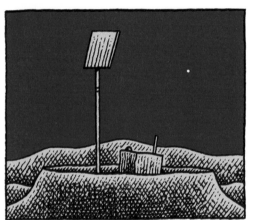

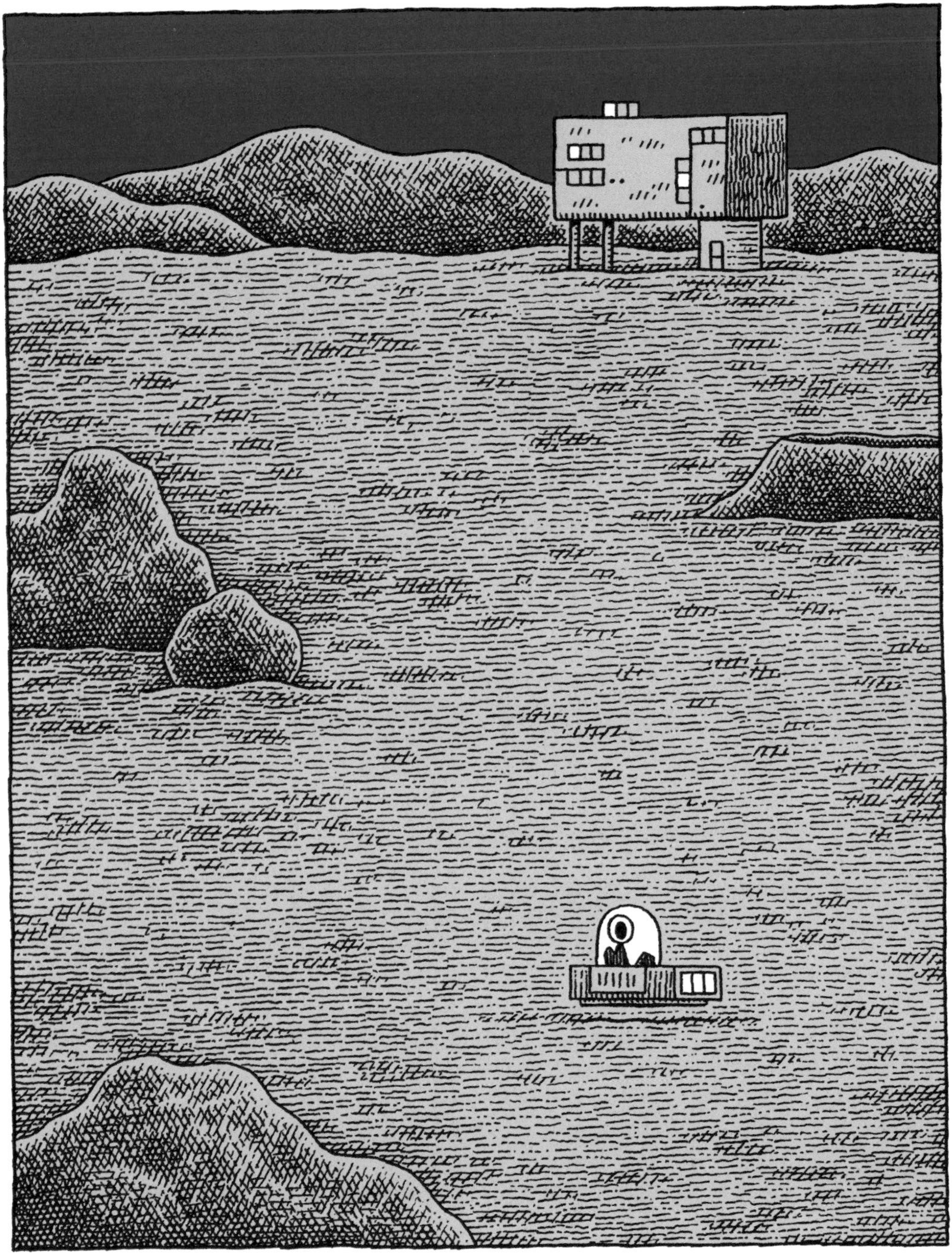

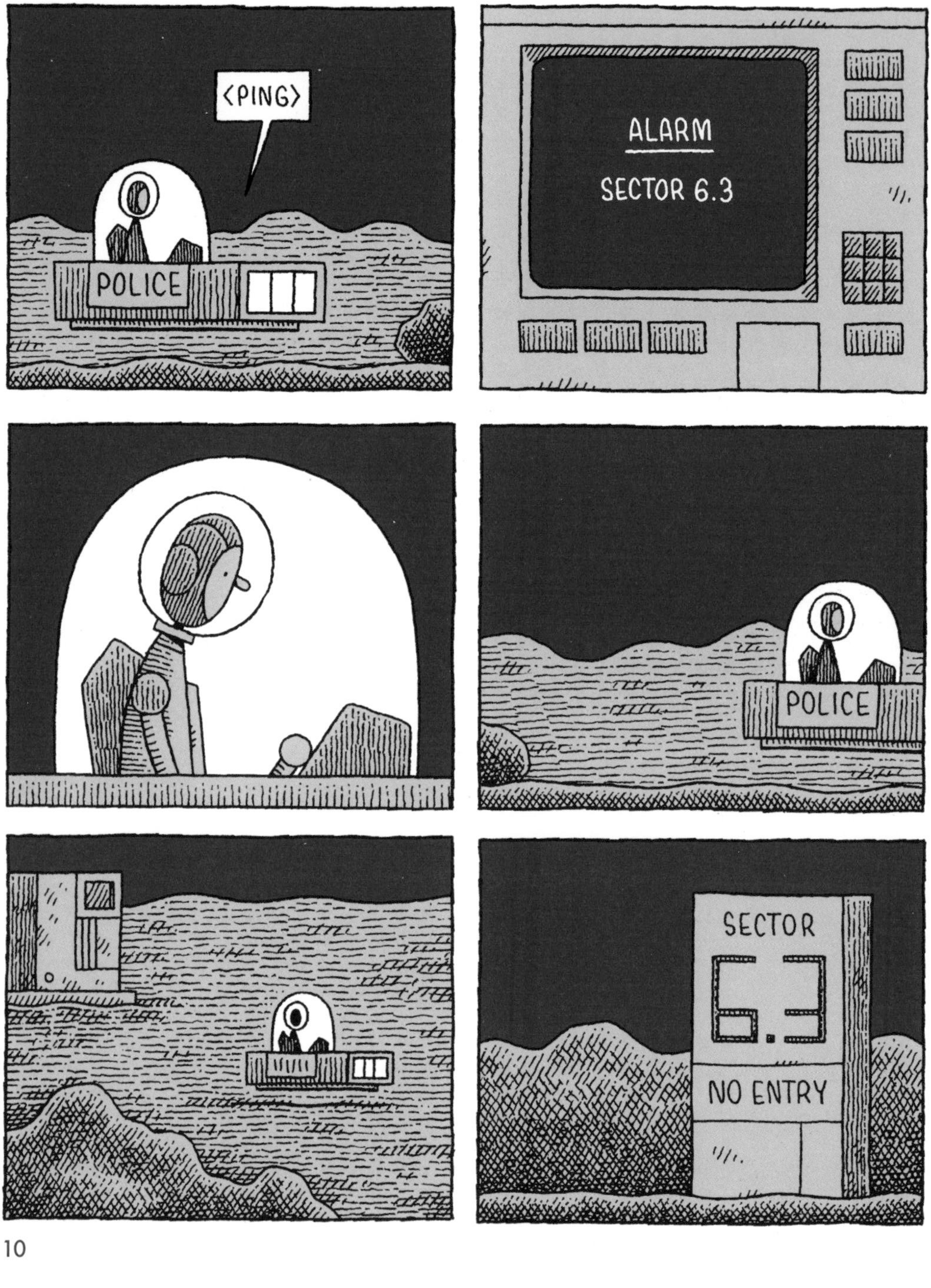
<PING>
POLICE
ALARM
SECTOR 6.3
POLICE
SECTOR
6.3
NO ENTRY

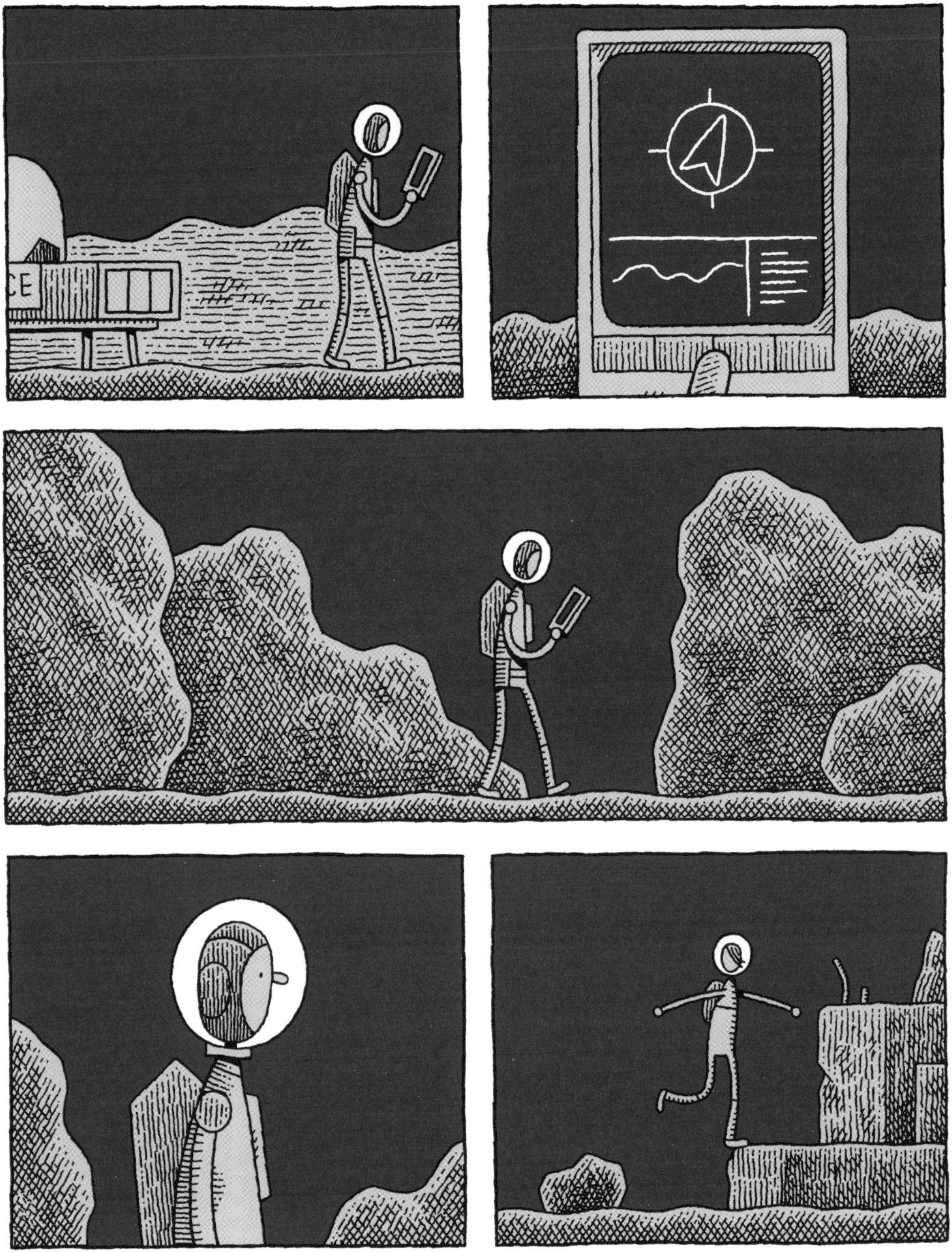
CE

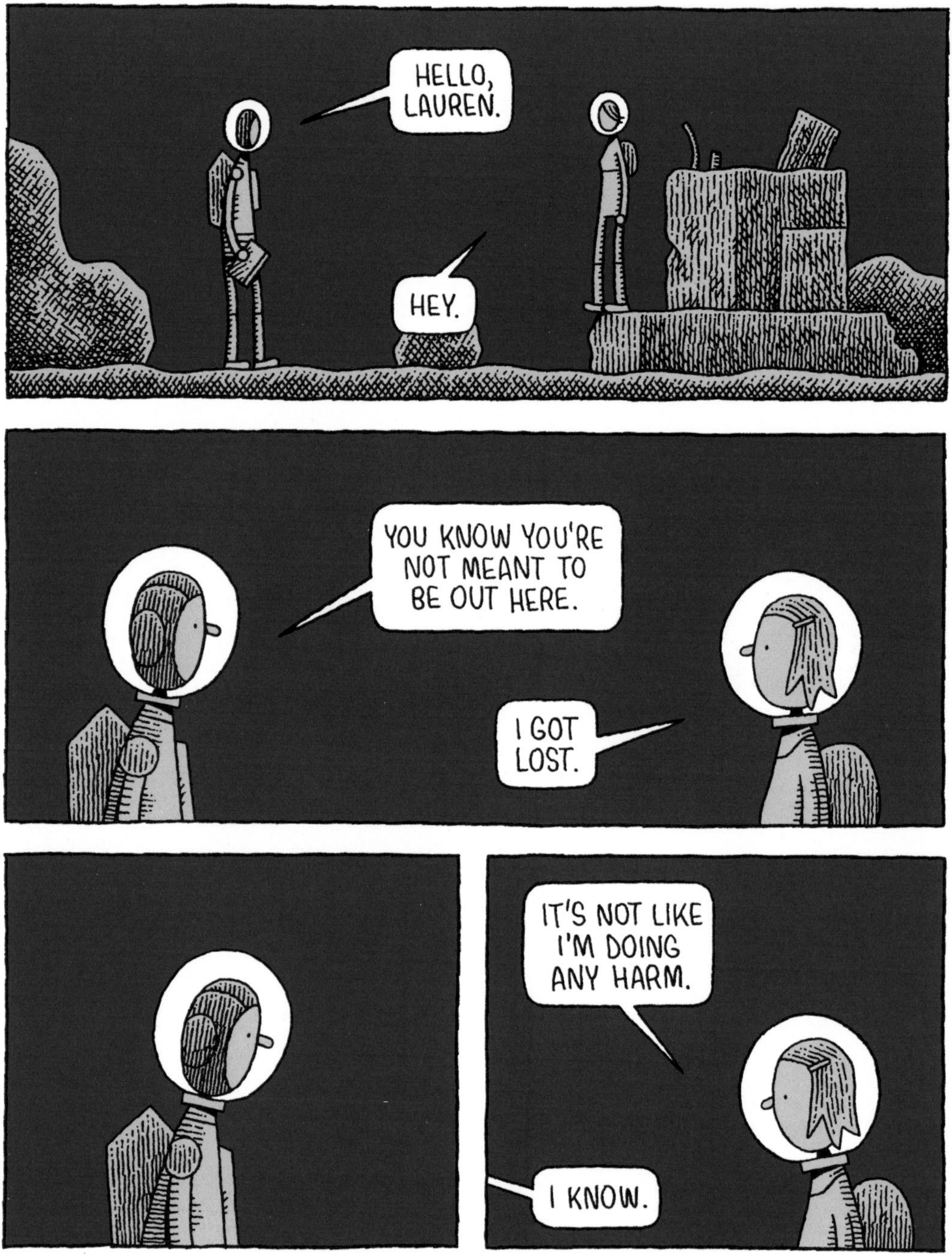
HELLO, LAUREN.
HEY.
YOU KNOW YOU'RE NOT MEANT TO BE OUT HERE.
I GOT LOST.
IT'S NOT LIKE I'M DOING ANY HARM.
I KNOW.

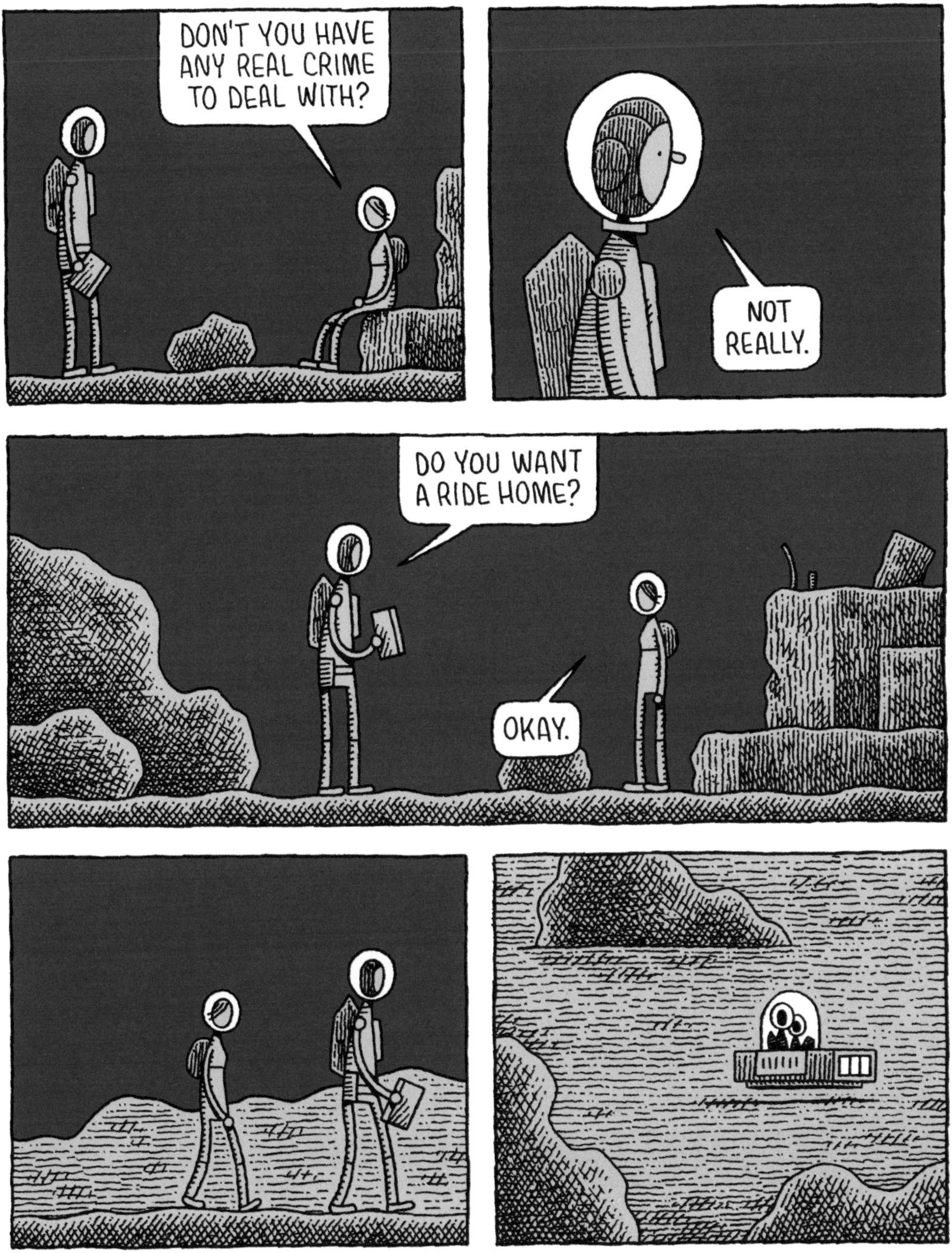
DON'T YOU HAVE ANY REAL CRIME TO DEAL WITH?
NOT REALLY.
DO YOU WANT A RIDE HOME?
OKAY.

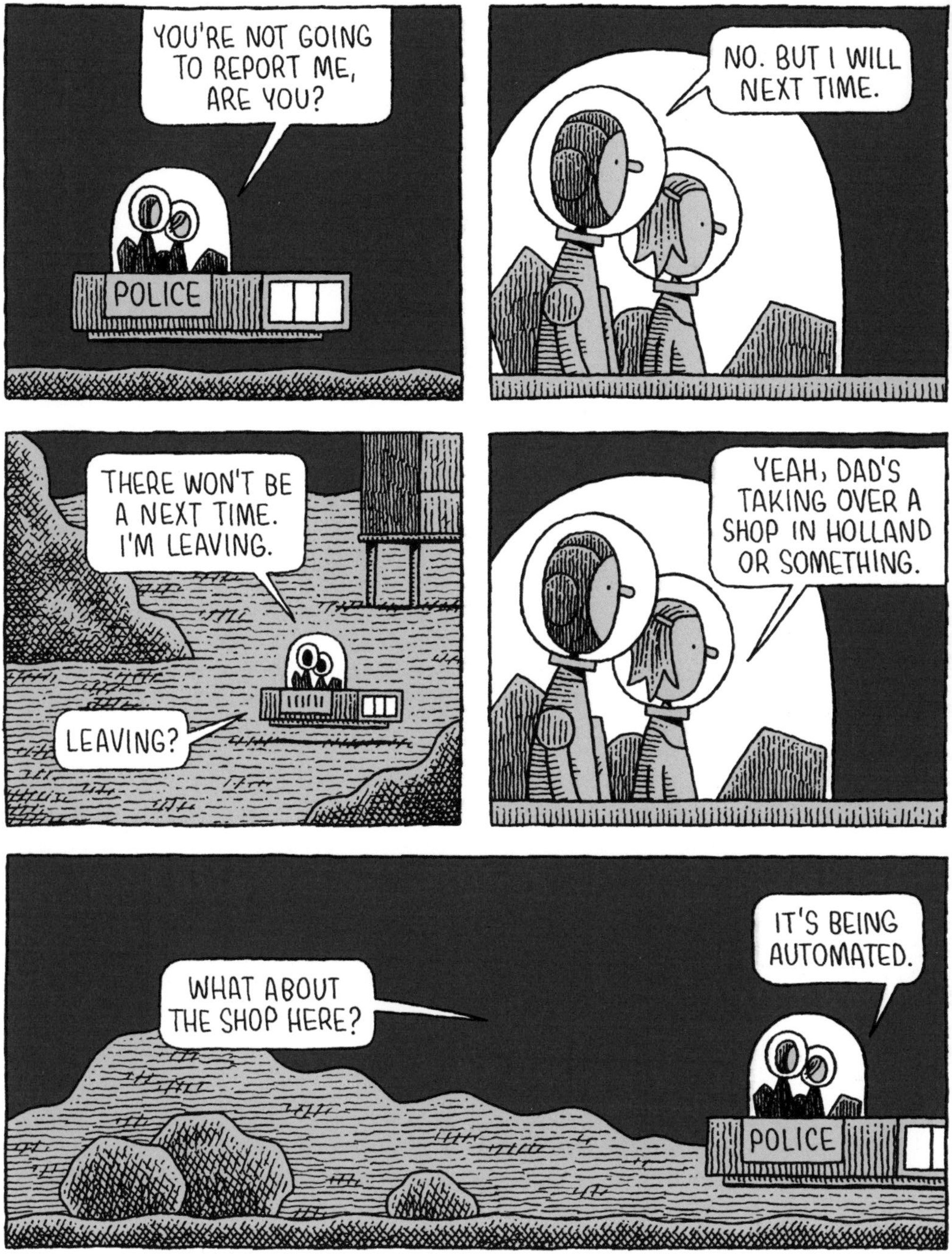
YOU'RE NOT GOING TO REPORT ME, ARE YOU?
POLICE
NO. BUT I WILL NEXT TIME.
THERE WON'T BE A NEXT TIME. I'M LEAVING.
LEAVING?
YEAH, DAD'S TAKING OVER A SHOP IN HOLLAND OR SOMETHING.
WHAT ABOUT THE SHOP HERE?
IT'S BEING AUTOMATED.
POLICE

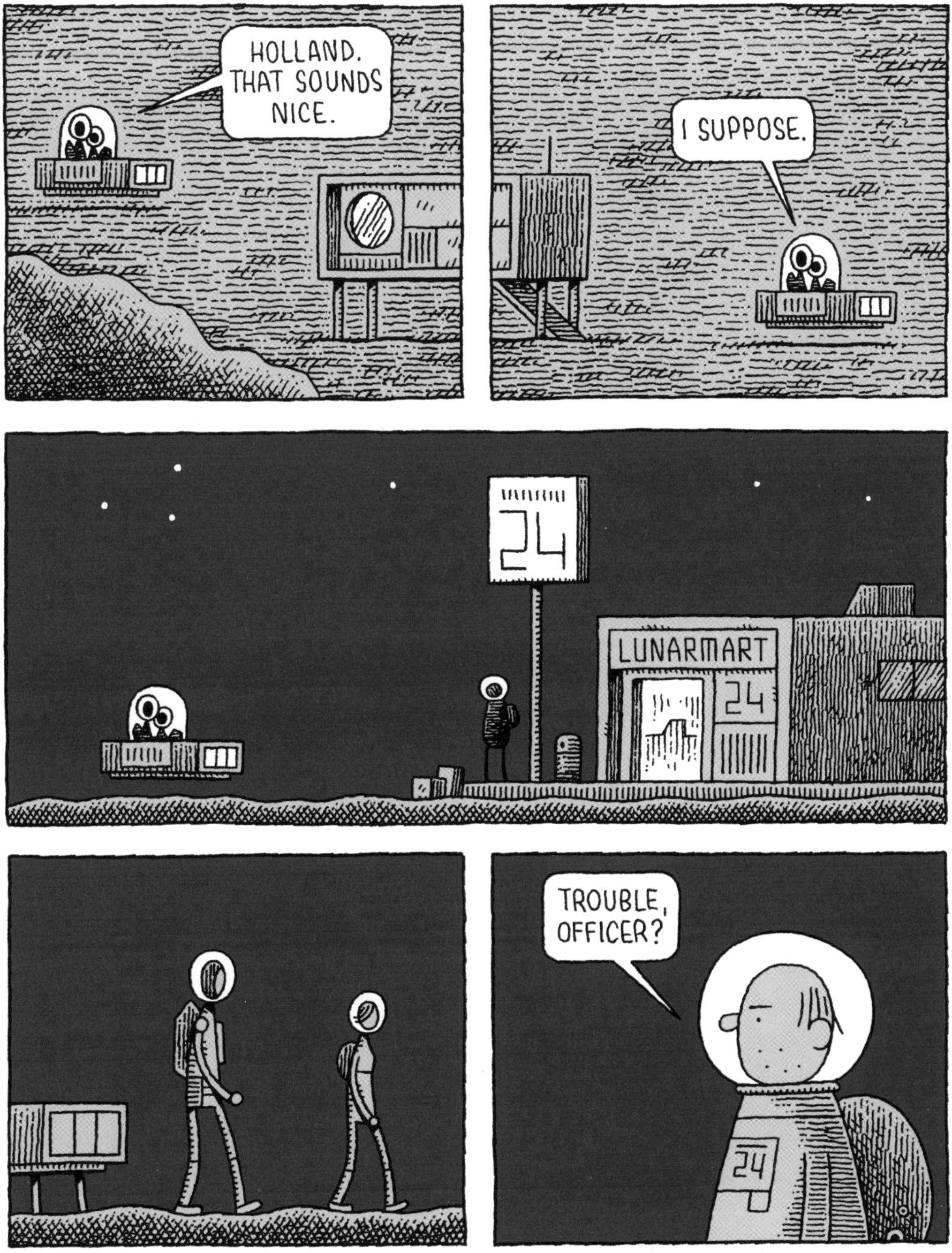
HOLLAND. THAT SOUNDS NICE.
I SUPPOSE.
24
LUNARMART
24
TROUBLE, OFFICER?
24

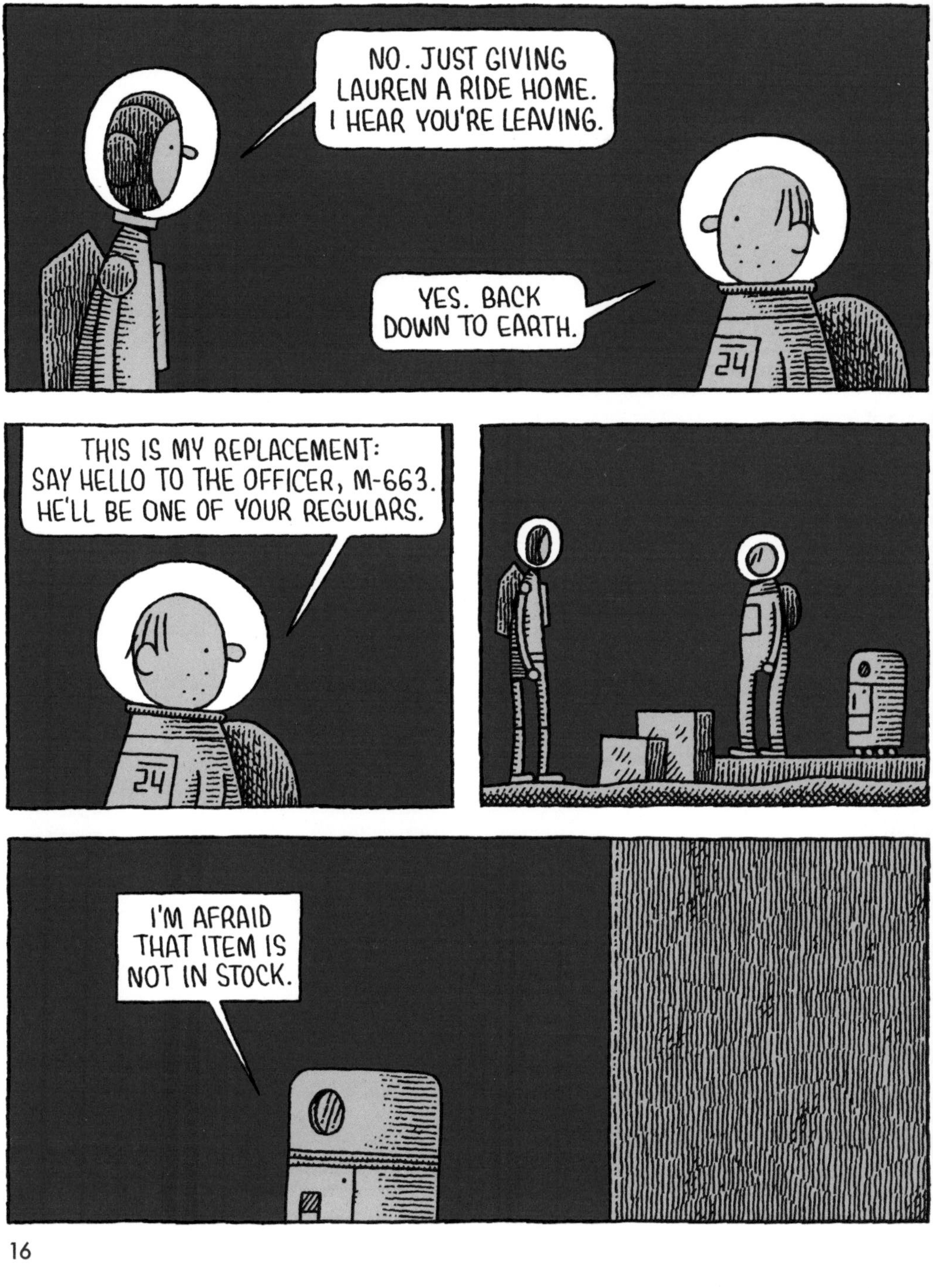
NO. JUST GIVING LAUREN A RIDE HOME. I HEAR YOU'RE LEAVING.
YES. BACK DOWN TO EARTH.
24
THIS IS MY REPLACEMENT: SAY HELLO TO THE OFFICER, M-663. HE'LL BE ONE OF YOUR REGULARS.
24
I'M AFRAID THAT ITEM IS NOT IN STOCK.

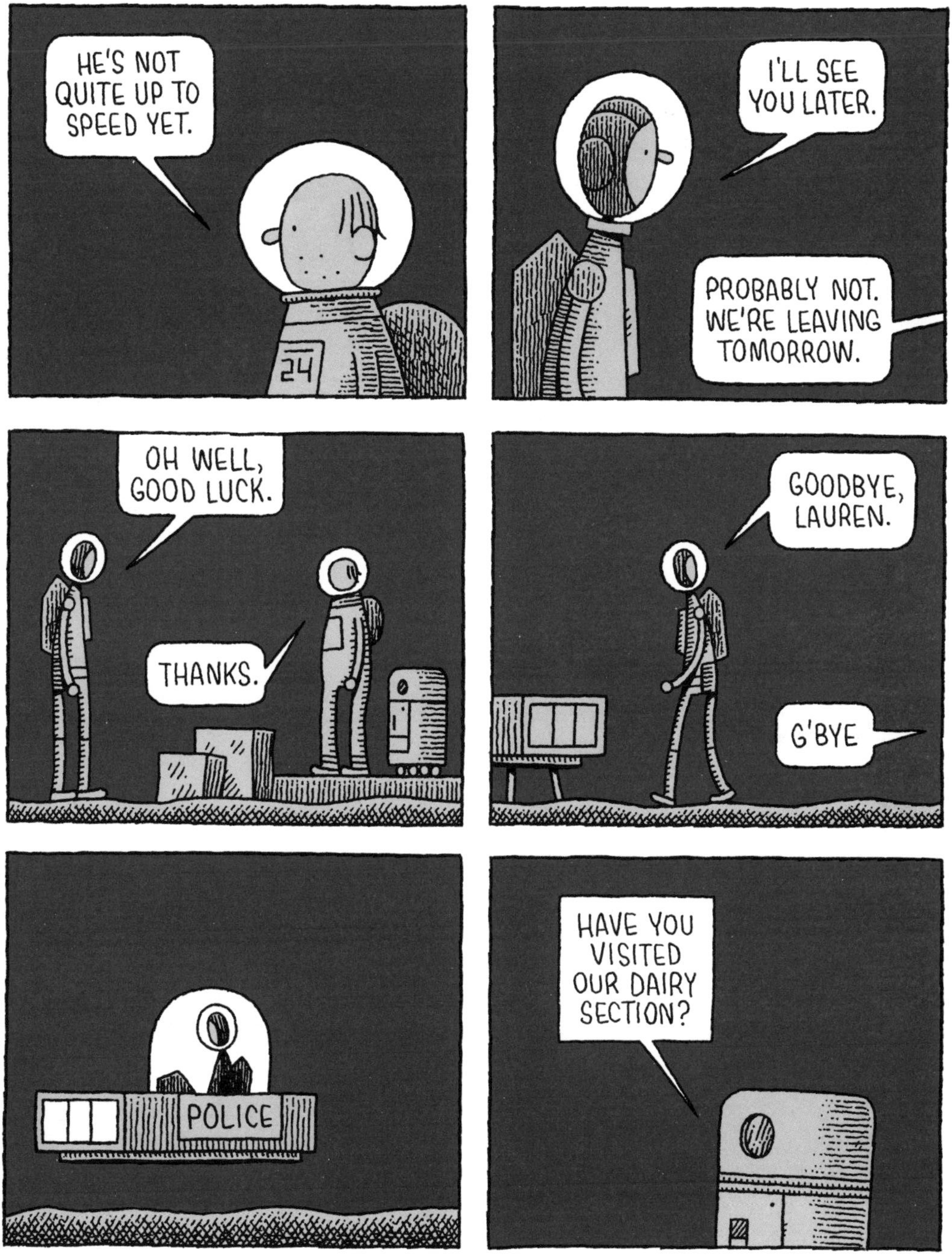

HE'S NOT QUITE UP TO SPEED YET.
I'LL SEE YOU LATER.
PROBABLY NOT. WE'RE LEAVING TOMORROW.
OH WELL, GOOD LUCK.
THANKS.
GOODBYE, LAUREN.
G'BYE
POLICE
HAVE YOU VISITED OUR DAIRY SECTION?

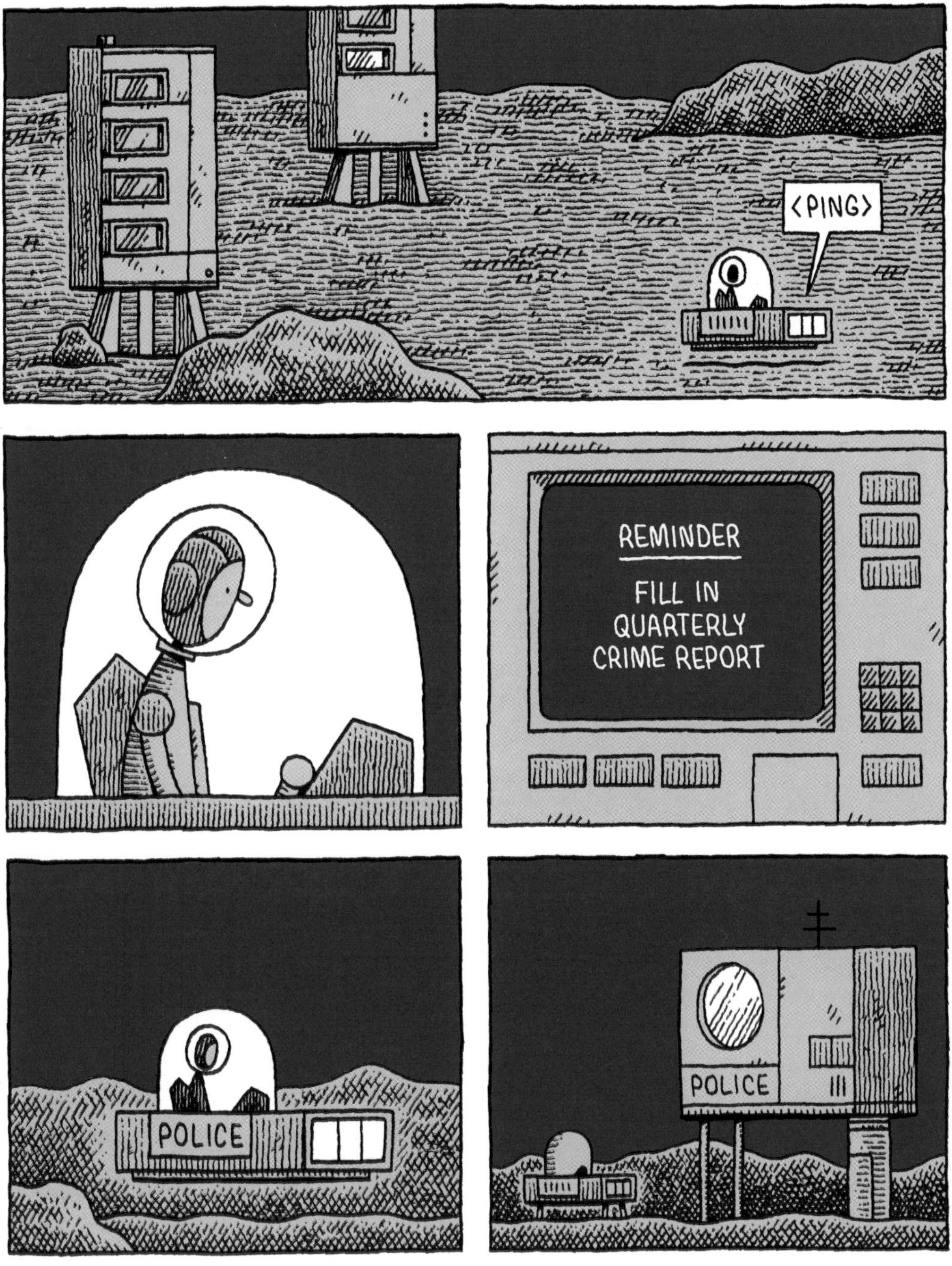
<PING>
REMINDER
FILL IN QUARTERLY CRIME REPORT
POLICE
POLICE
III

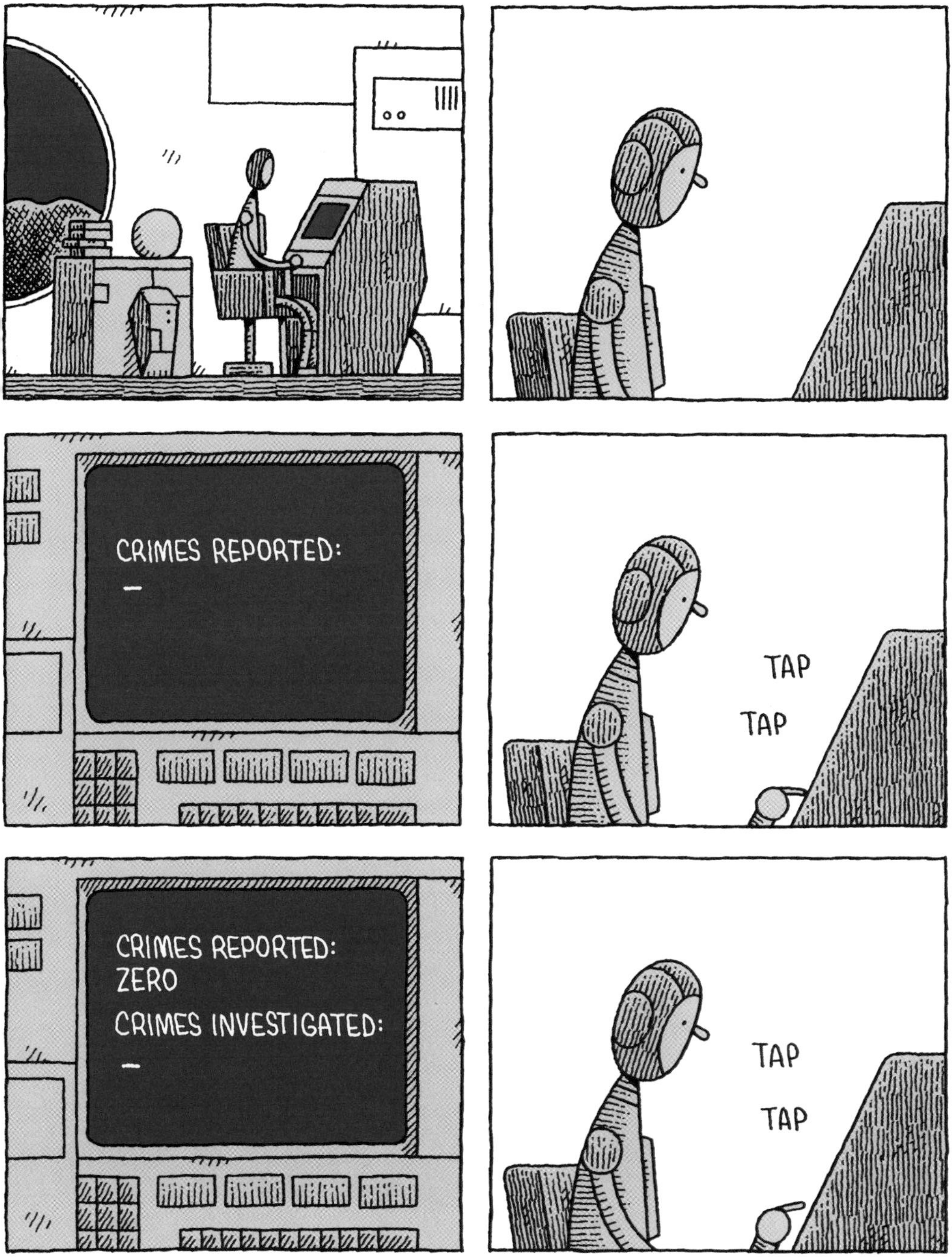
CRIMES REPORTED:
—
TAP
TAP
CRIMES REPORTED:
ZERO
CRIMES INVESTIGATED:
—
TAP
TAP

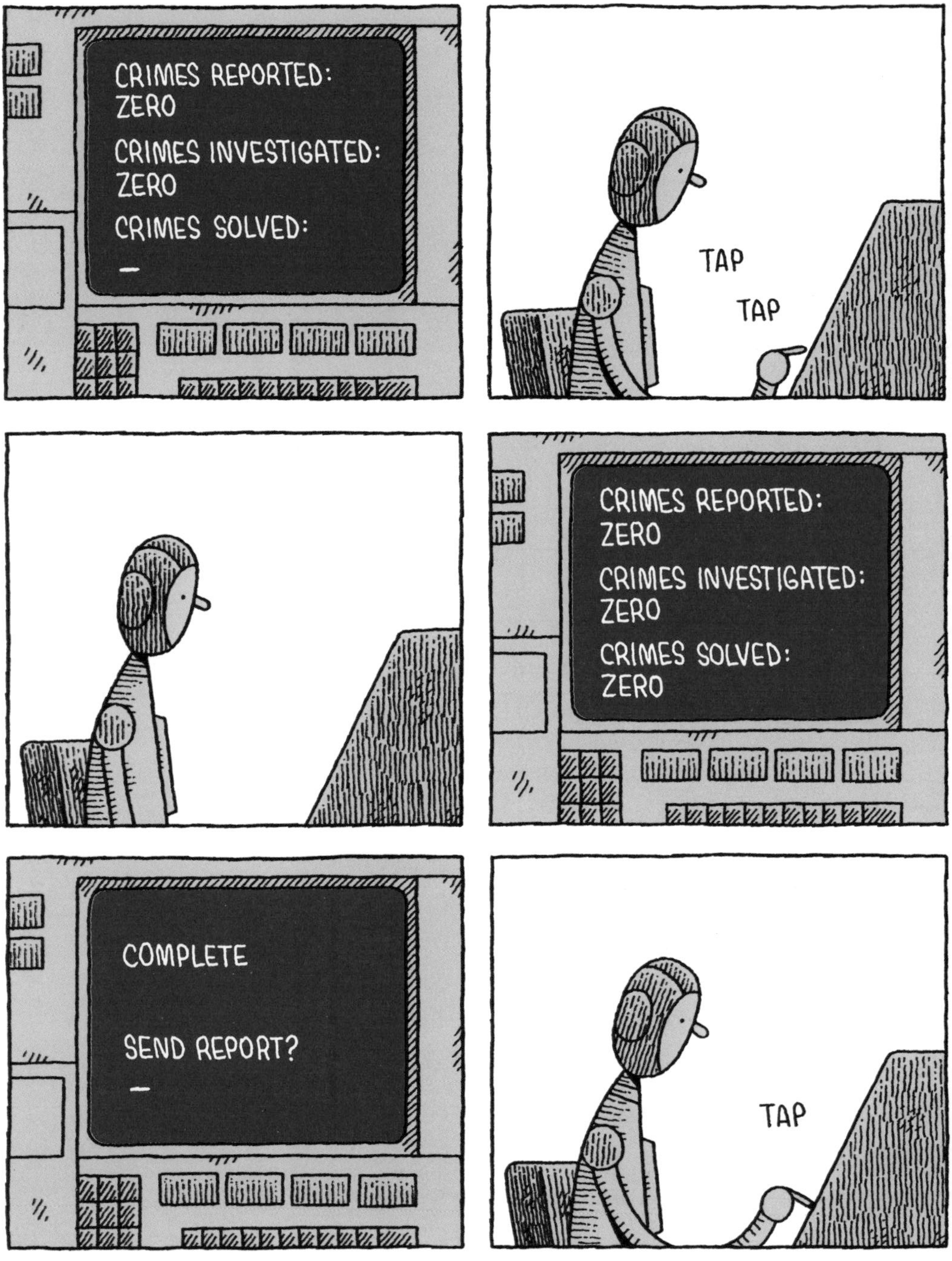
CRIMES REPORTED:
ZERO
CRIMES INVESTIGATED:
ZERO
CRIMES SOLVED:
TAP
TAP
CRIMES REPORTED:
ZERO
CRIMES INVESTIGATED:
ZERO
CRIMES SOLVED:
ZERO
COMPLETE
SEND REPORT?
TAP

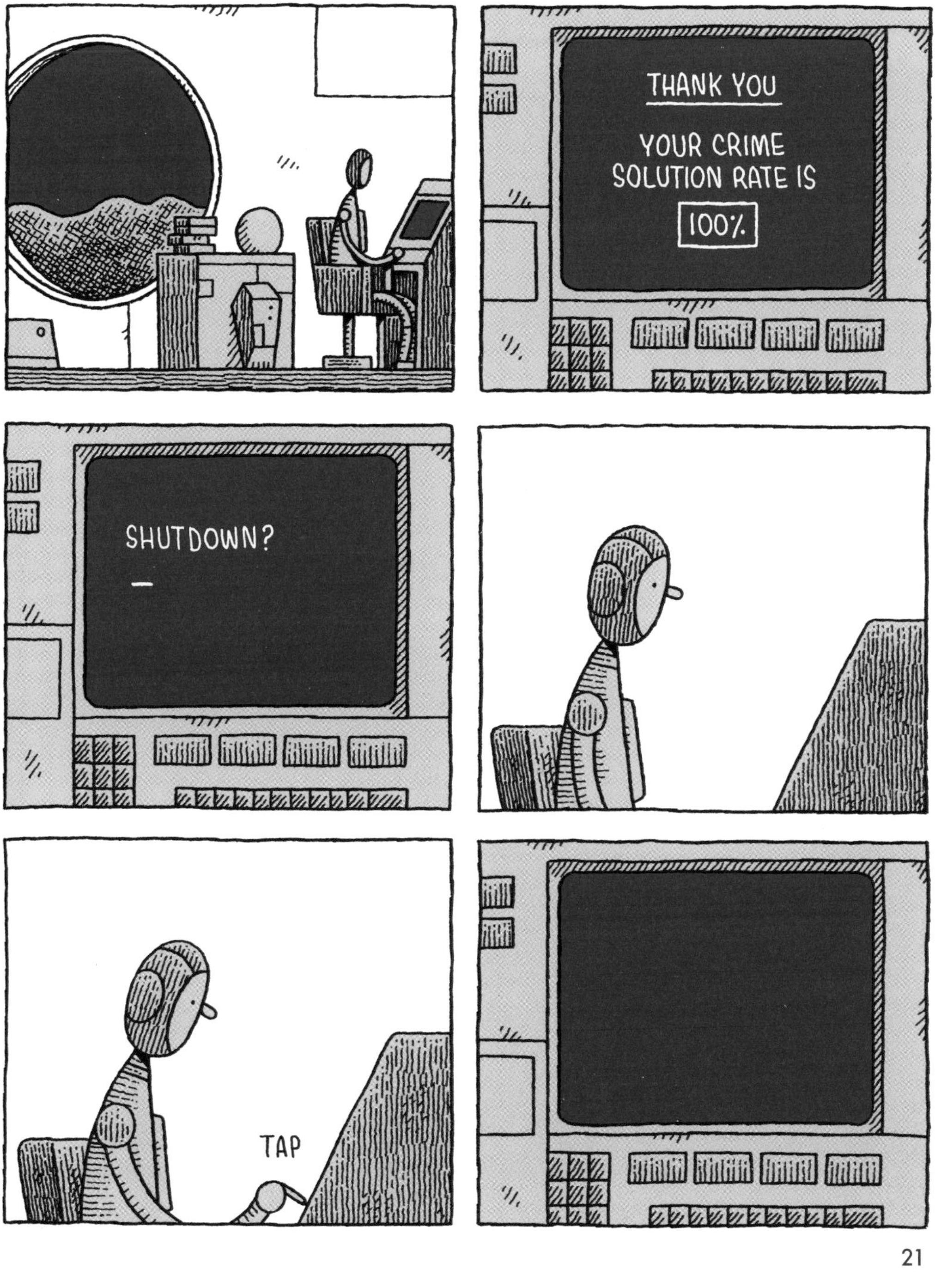
THANK YOU
YOUR CRIME SOLUTION RATE IS
100%
SHUTDOWN?
TAP

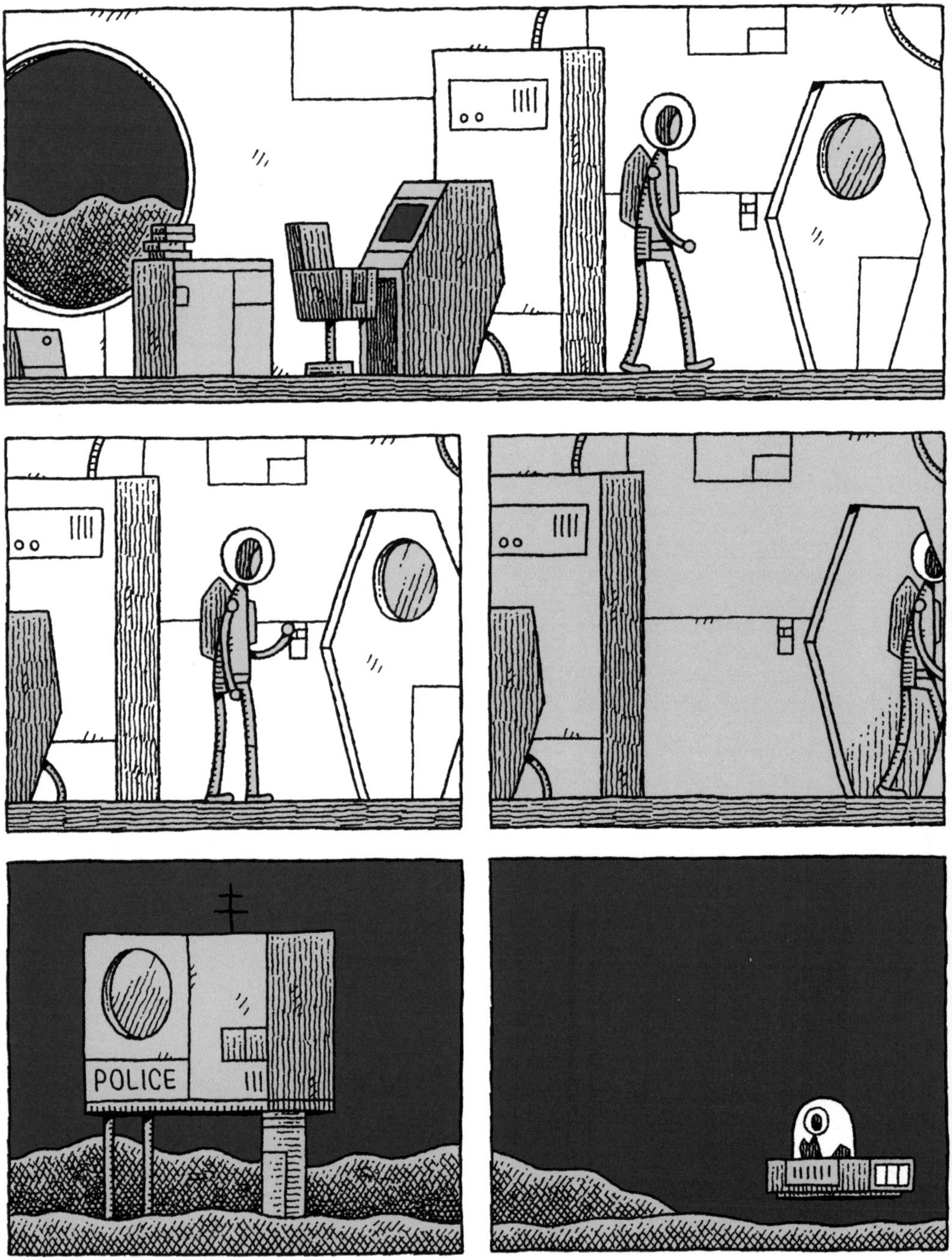
POLICE

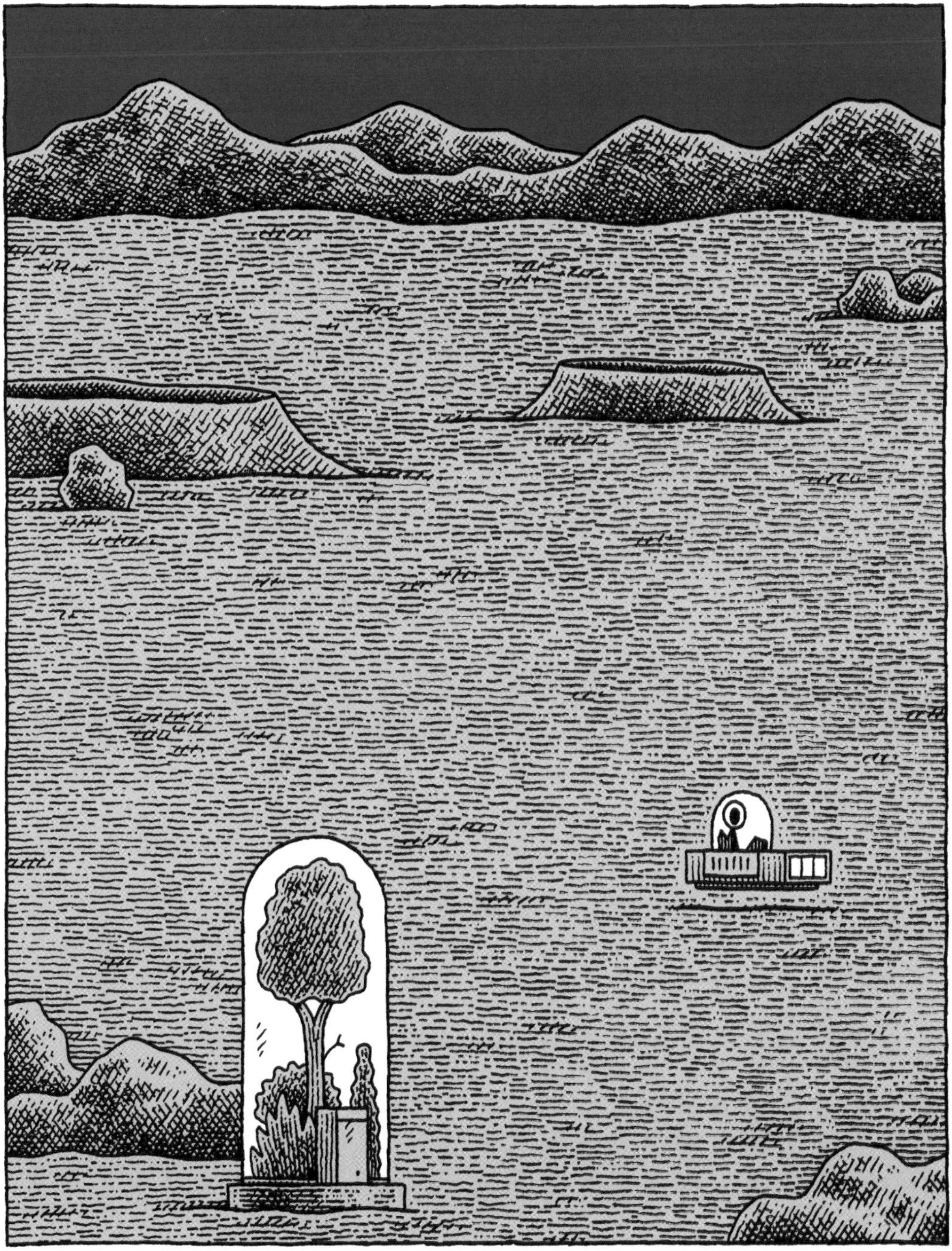

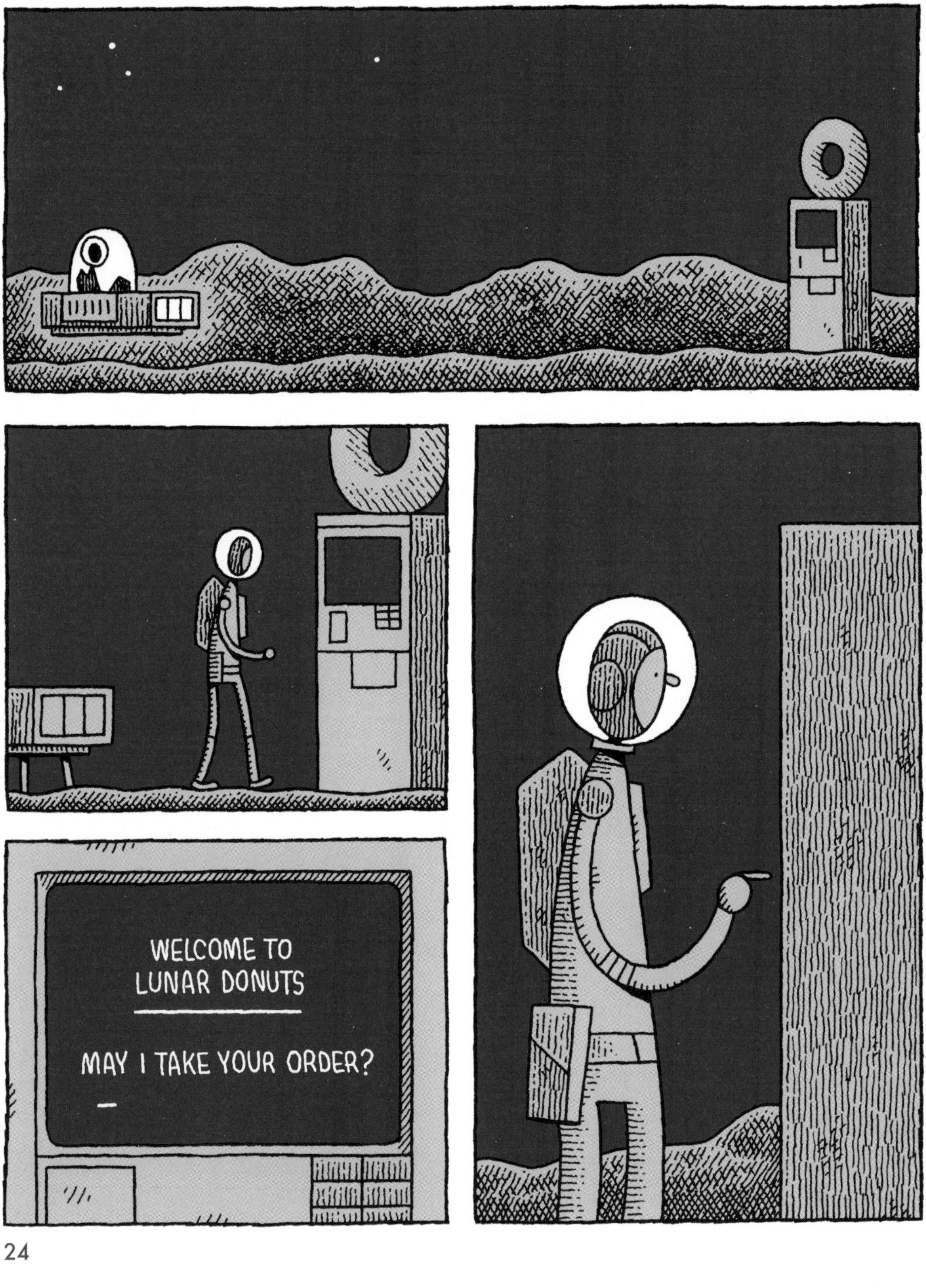
WELCOME TO
LUNAR DONUTS
MAY I TAKE YOUR ORDER?

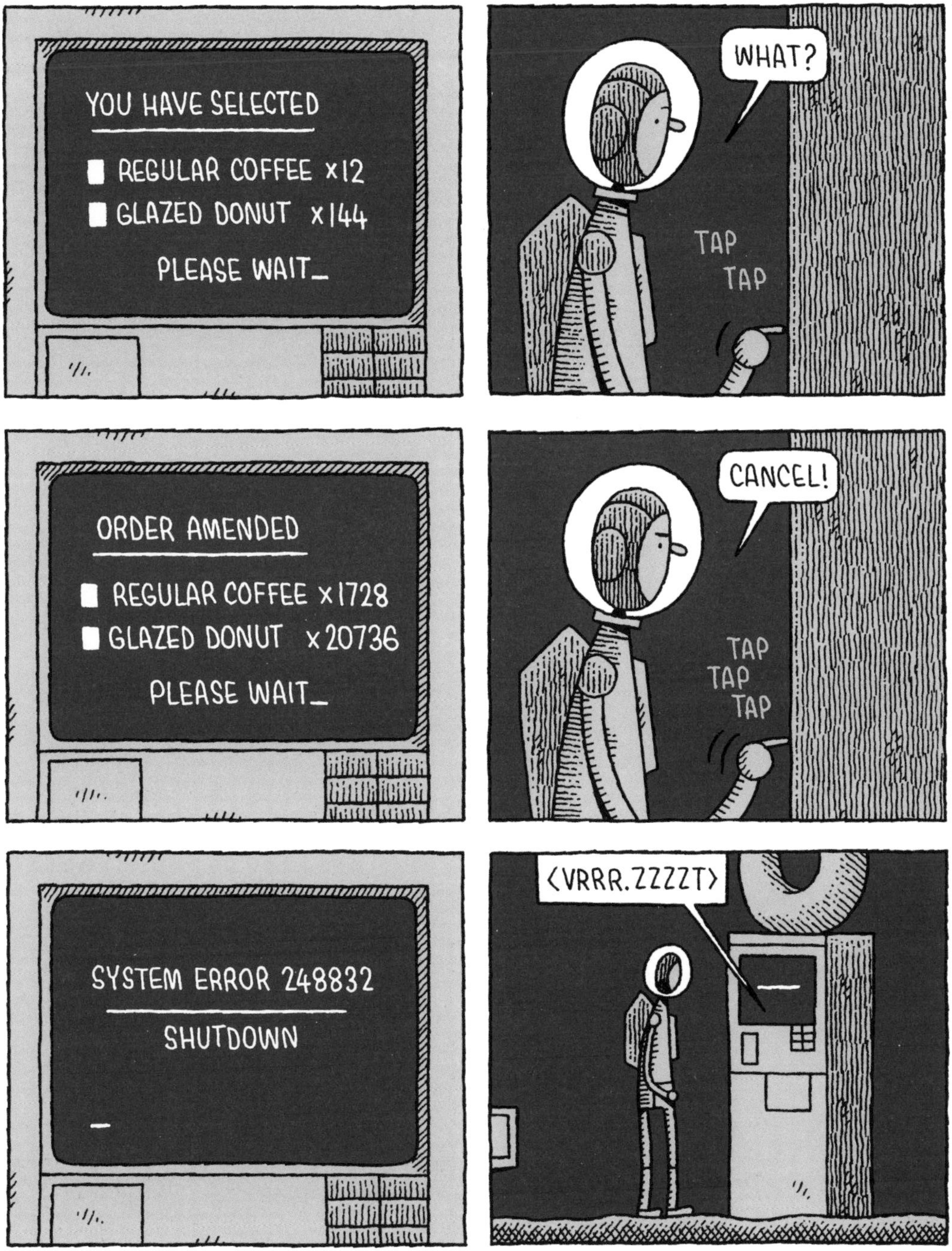
YOU HAVE SELECTED
REGULAR COFFEE x12
GLAZED DONUT x144
PLEASE WAIT_
WHAT?
TAP TAP
ORDER AMENDED
REGULAR COFFEE x1728
GLAZED DONUT x20736
PLEASE WAIT_
CANCEL!
TAP TAP TAP
SYSTEM ERROR 248832
SHUTDOWN
<VRRR.ZZZZT>

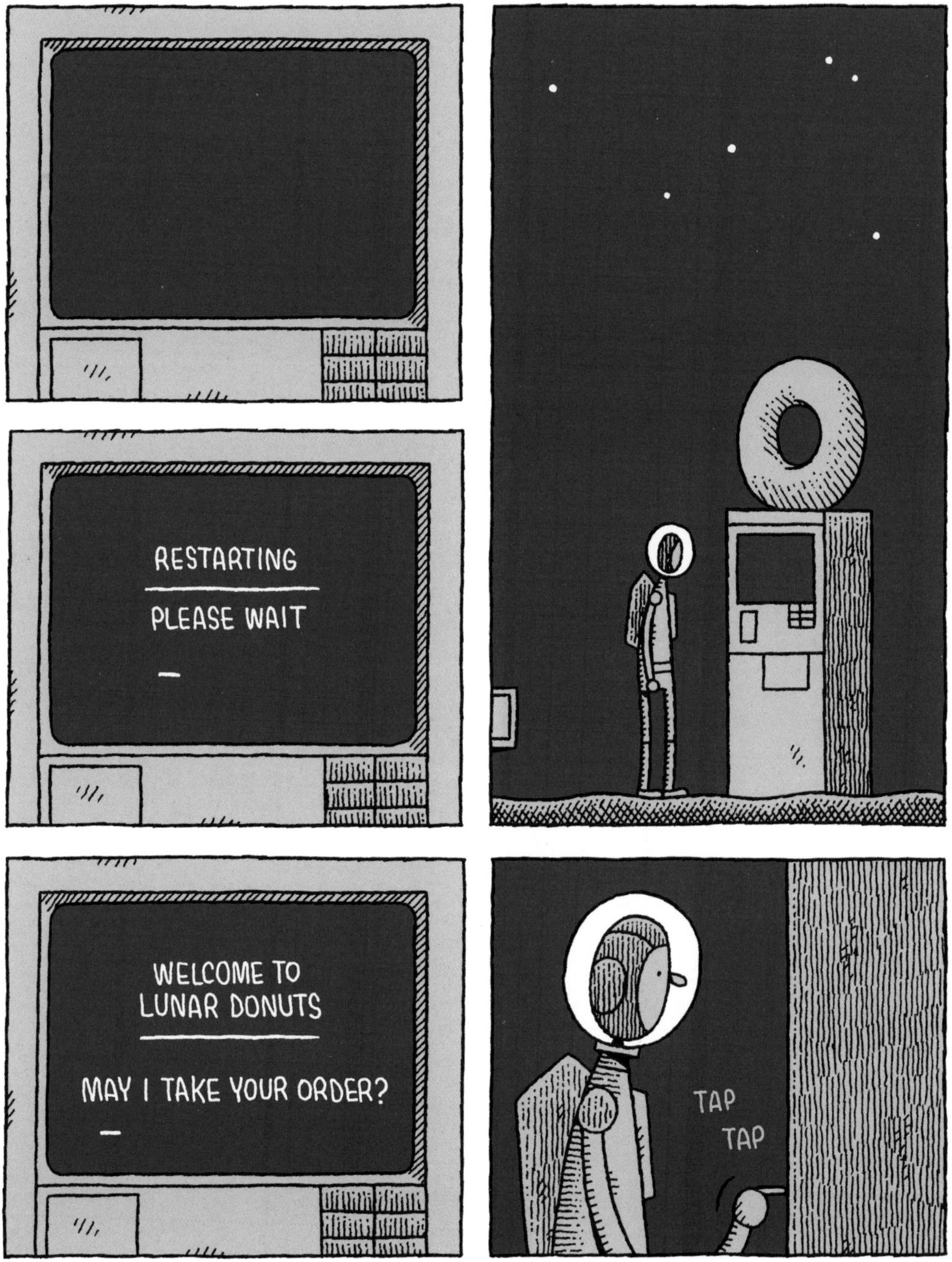
RESTARTING
PLEASE WAIT
WELCOME TO LUNAR DONUTS
MAY I TAKE YOUR ORDER?
TAP
TAP

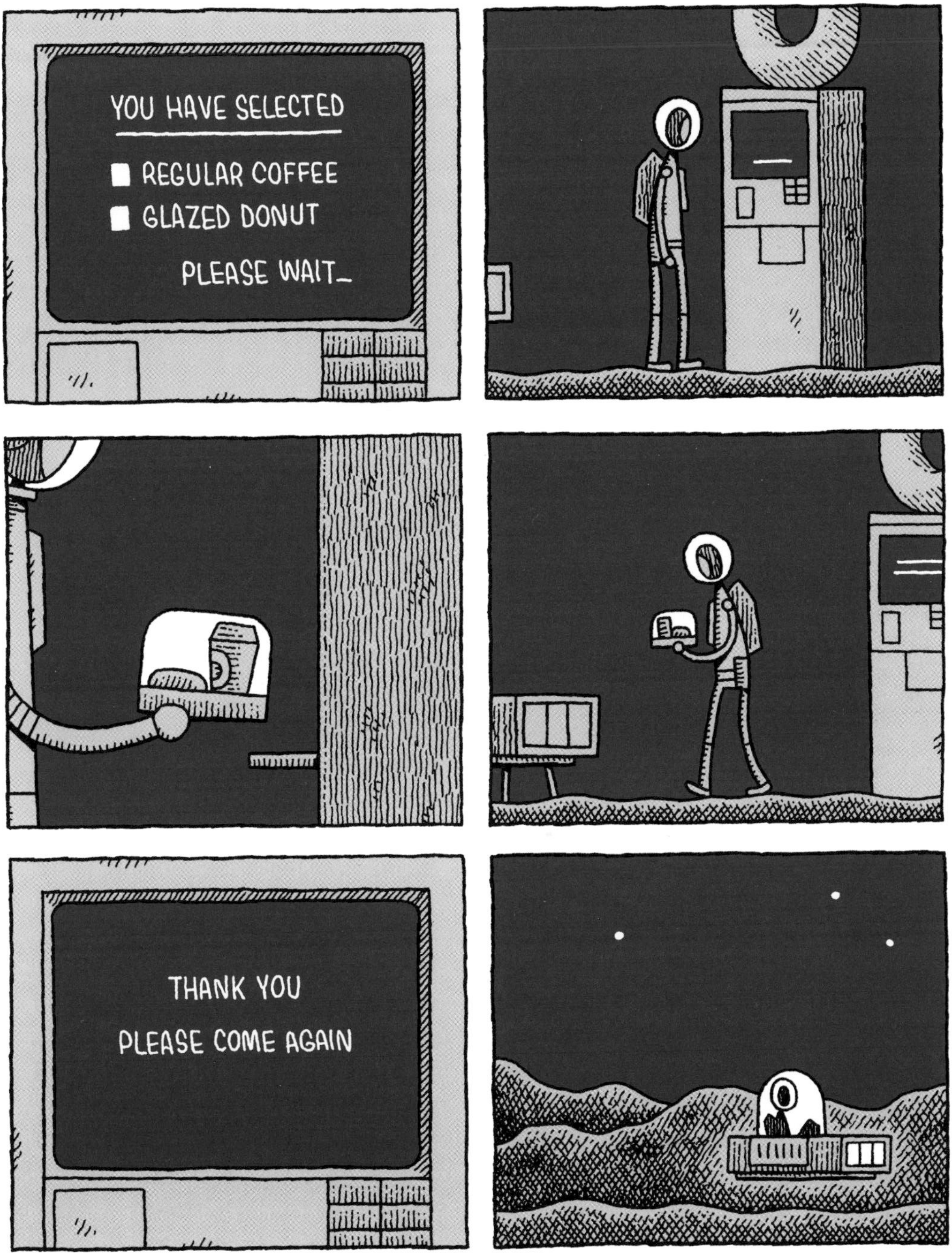
YOU HAVE SELECTED
REGULAR COFFEE
GLAZED DONUT
PLEASE WAIT_
THANK YOU
PLEASE COME AGAIN

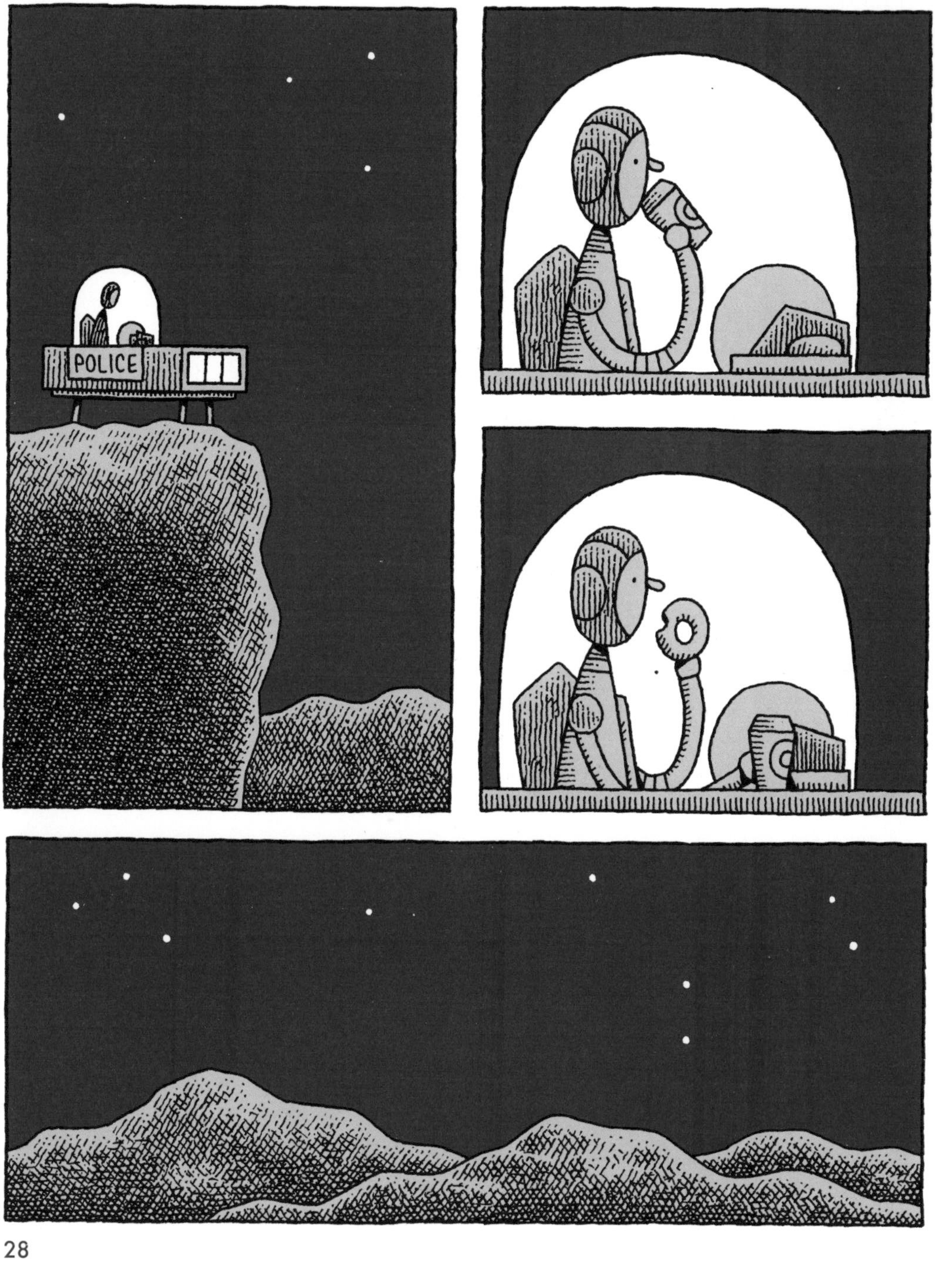
POLICE

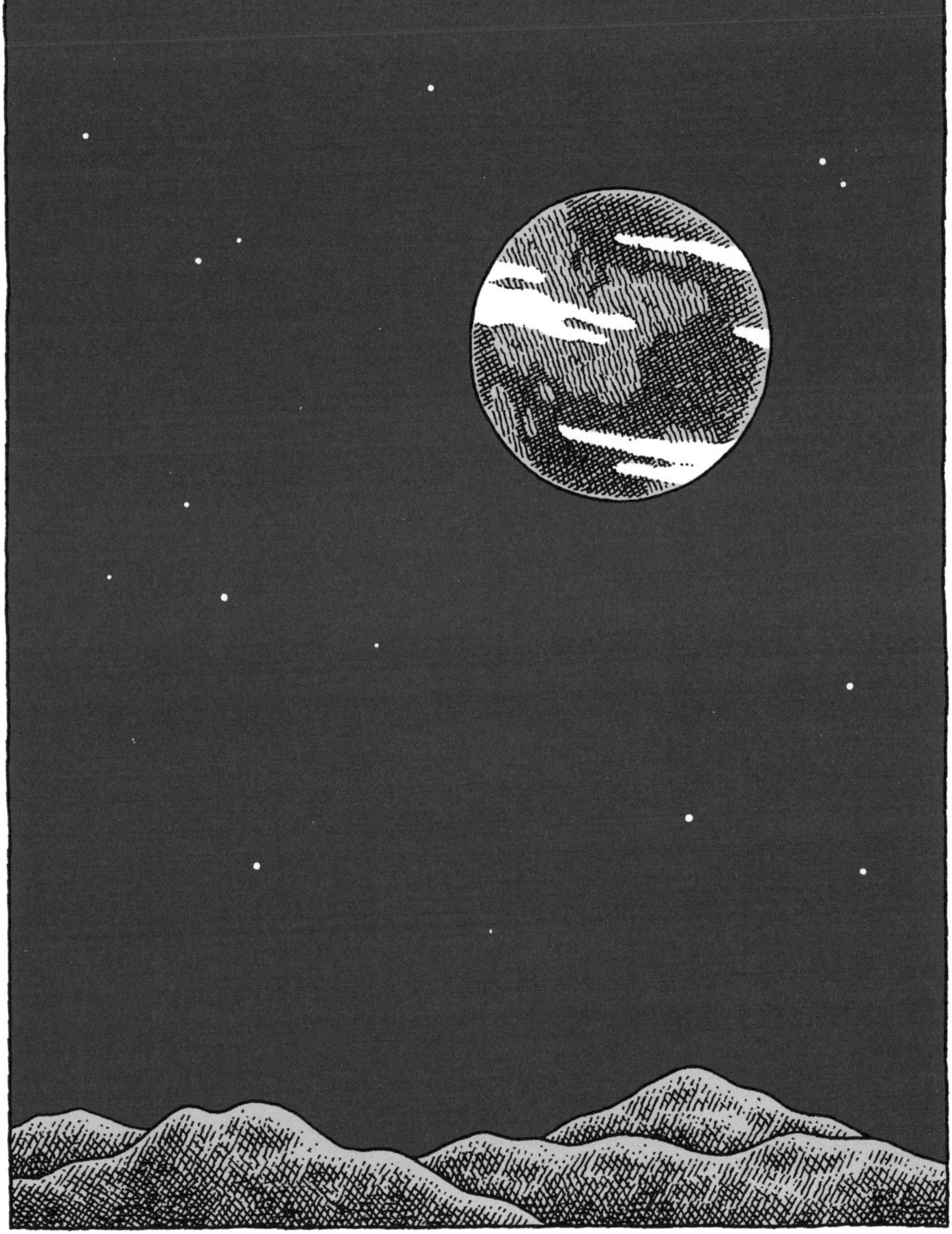

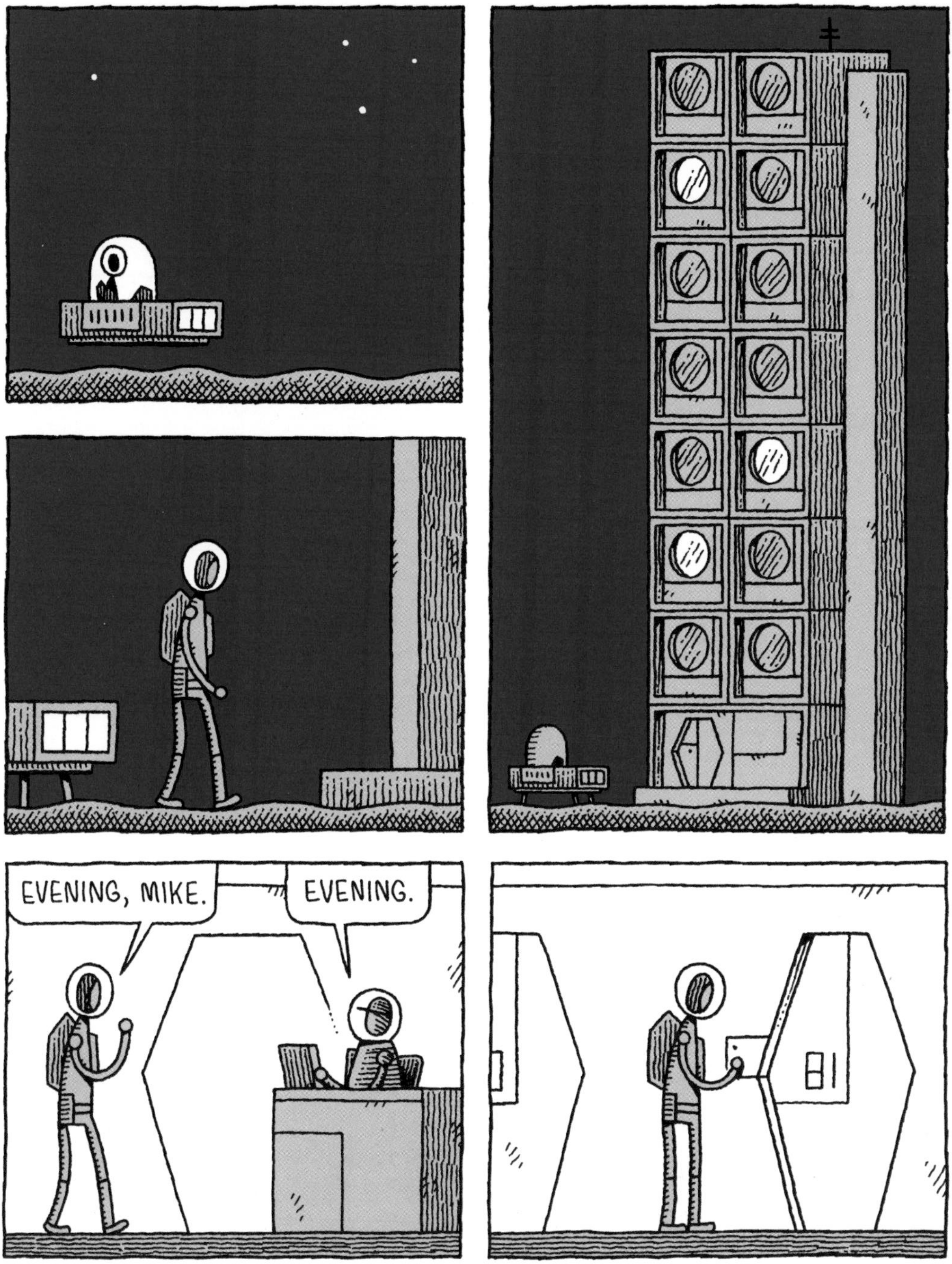
EVENING, MIKE.
EVENING.
B1

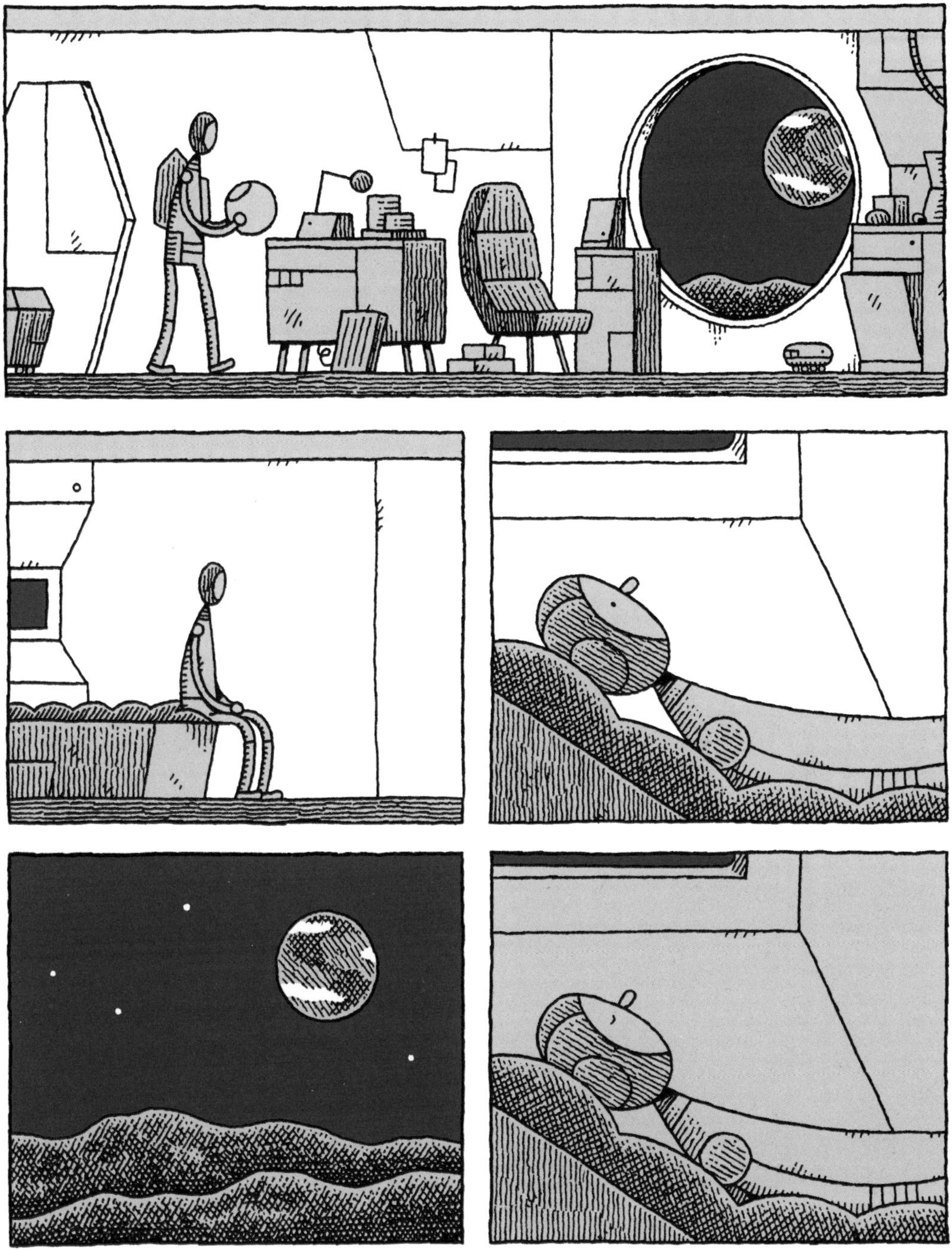

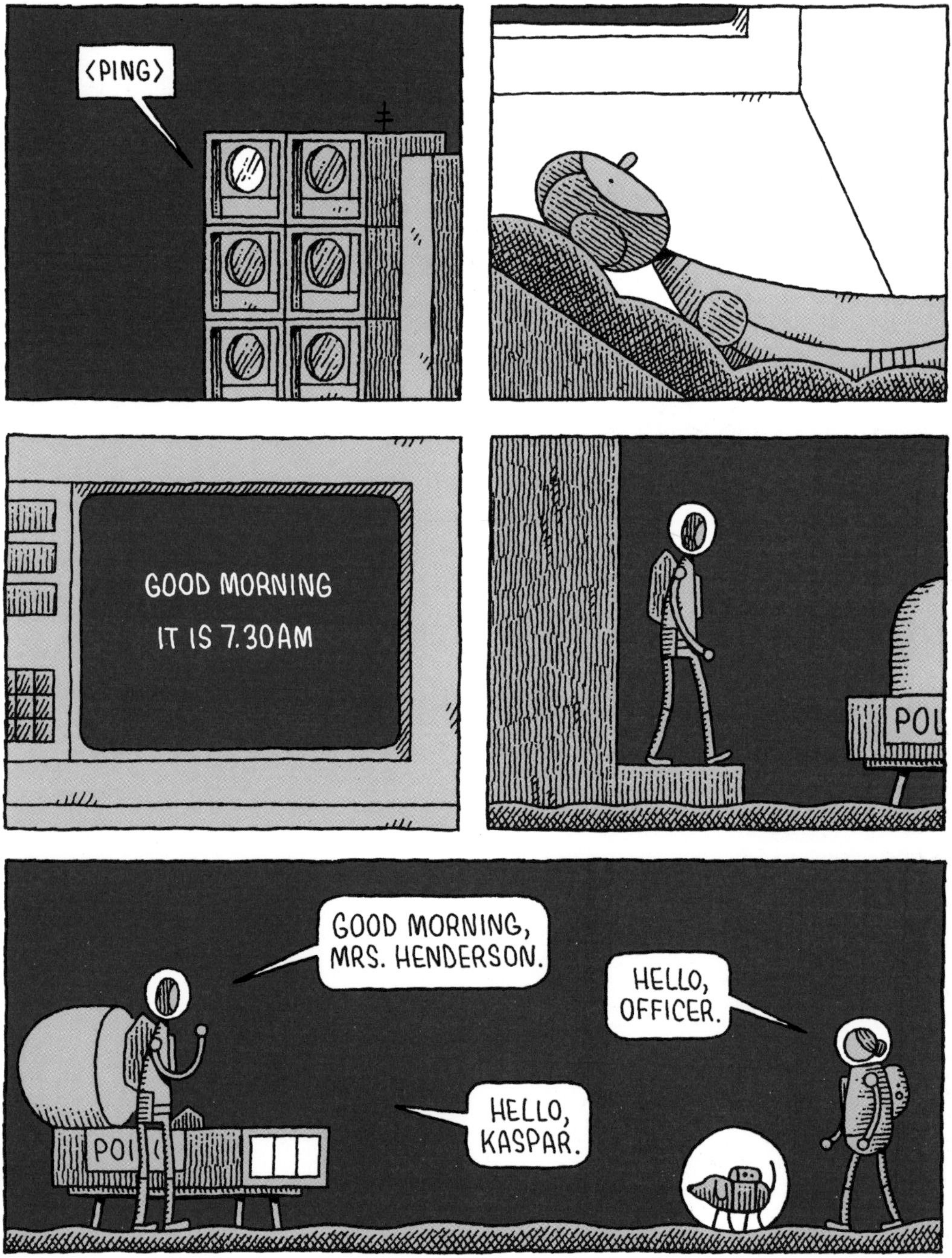
<PING>
GOOD MORNING
IT IS 7.30AM
POL
GOOD MORNING, MRS. HENDERSON.
HELLO, OFFICER.
HELLO, KASPAR.
POI

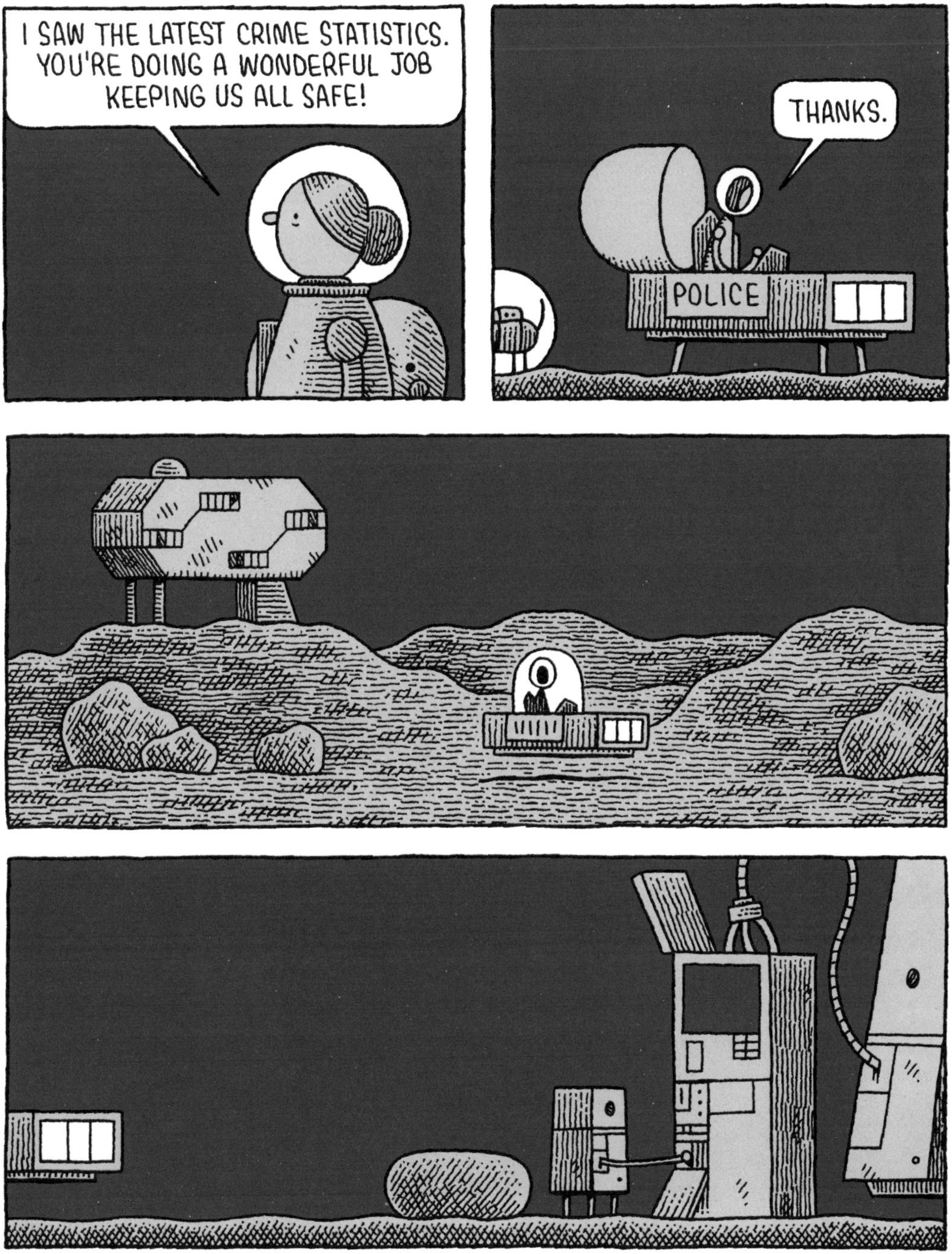
I SAW THE LATEST CRIME STATISTICS. YOU'RE DOING A WONDERFUL JOB KEEPING US ALL SAFE!
THANKS.
POLICE

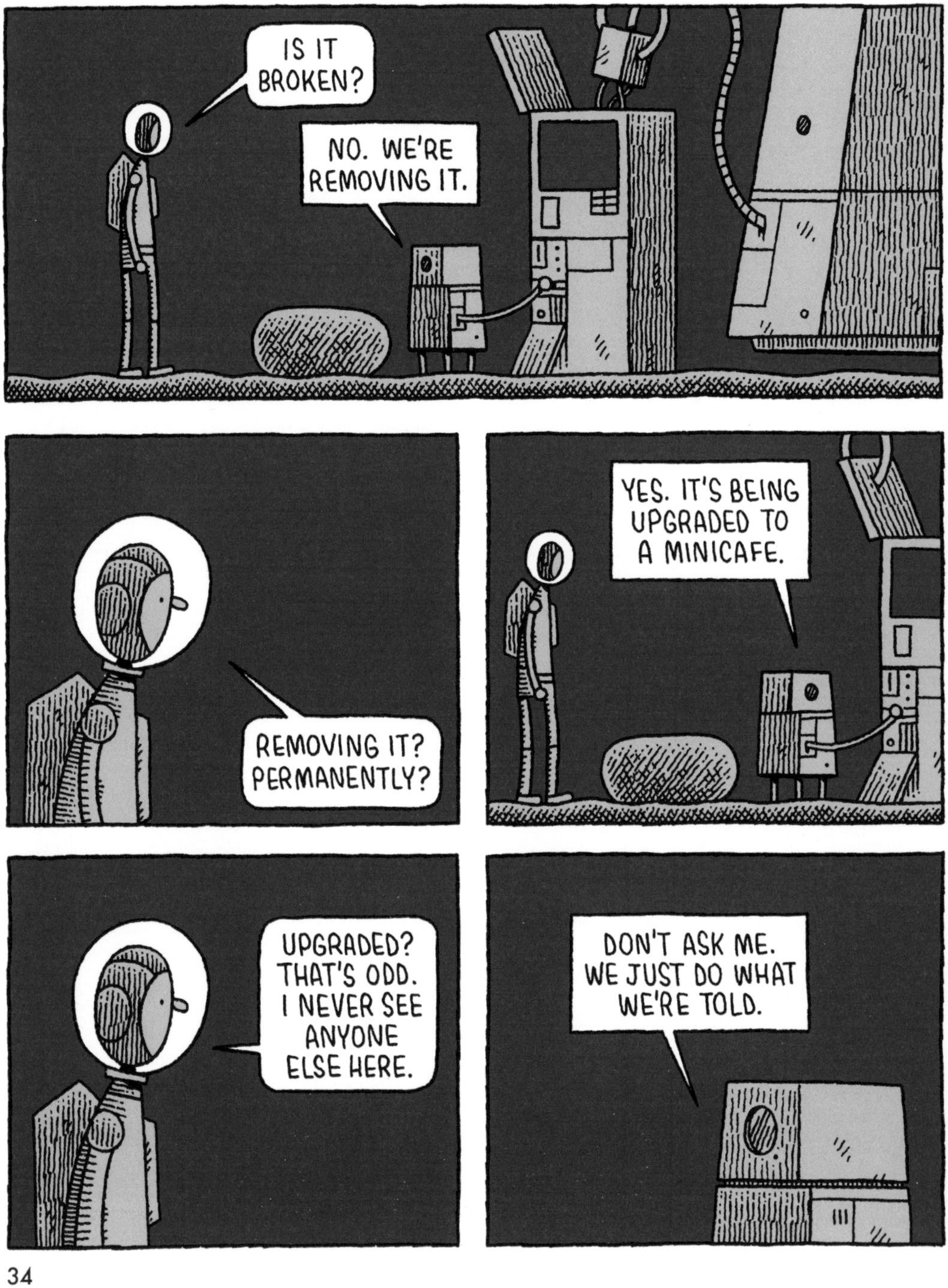
IS IT BROKEN?
NO. WE'RE REMOVING IT.
REMOVING IT? PERMANENTLY?
YES. IT'S BEING UPGRADED TO A MINICAFE.
UPGRADED? THAT'S ODD. I NEVER SEE ANYONE ELSE HERE.
DON'T ASK ME. WE JUST DO WHAT WE'RE TOLD.

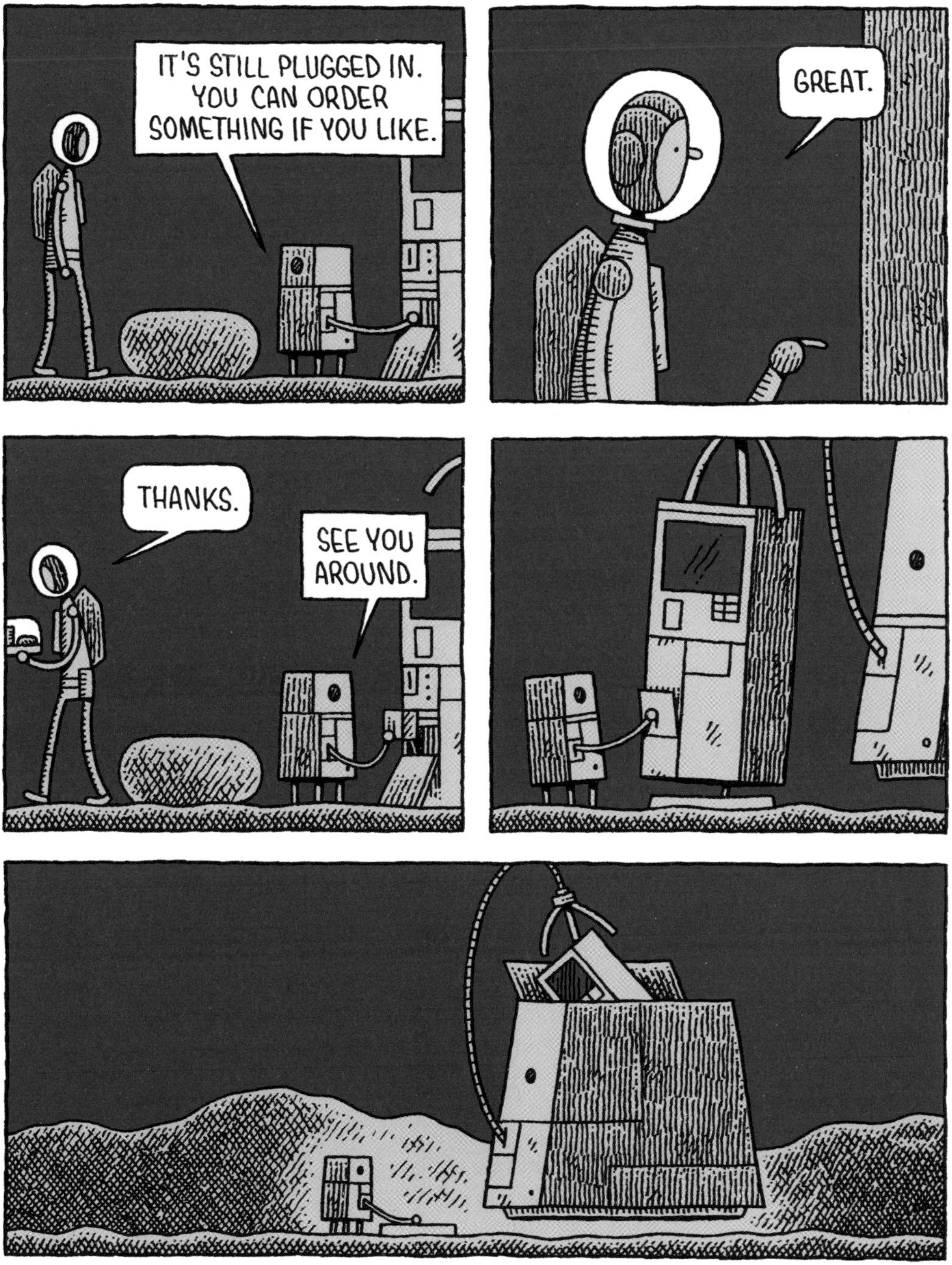
IT'S STILL PLUGGED IN. YOU CAN ORDER SOMETHING IF YOU LIKE.
GREAT.
THANKS.
SEE YOU AROUND.

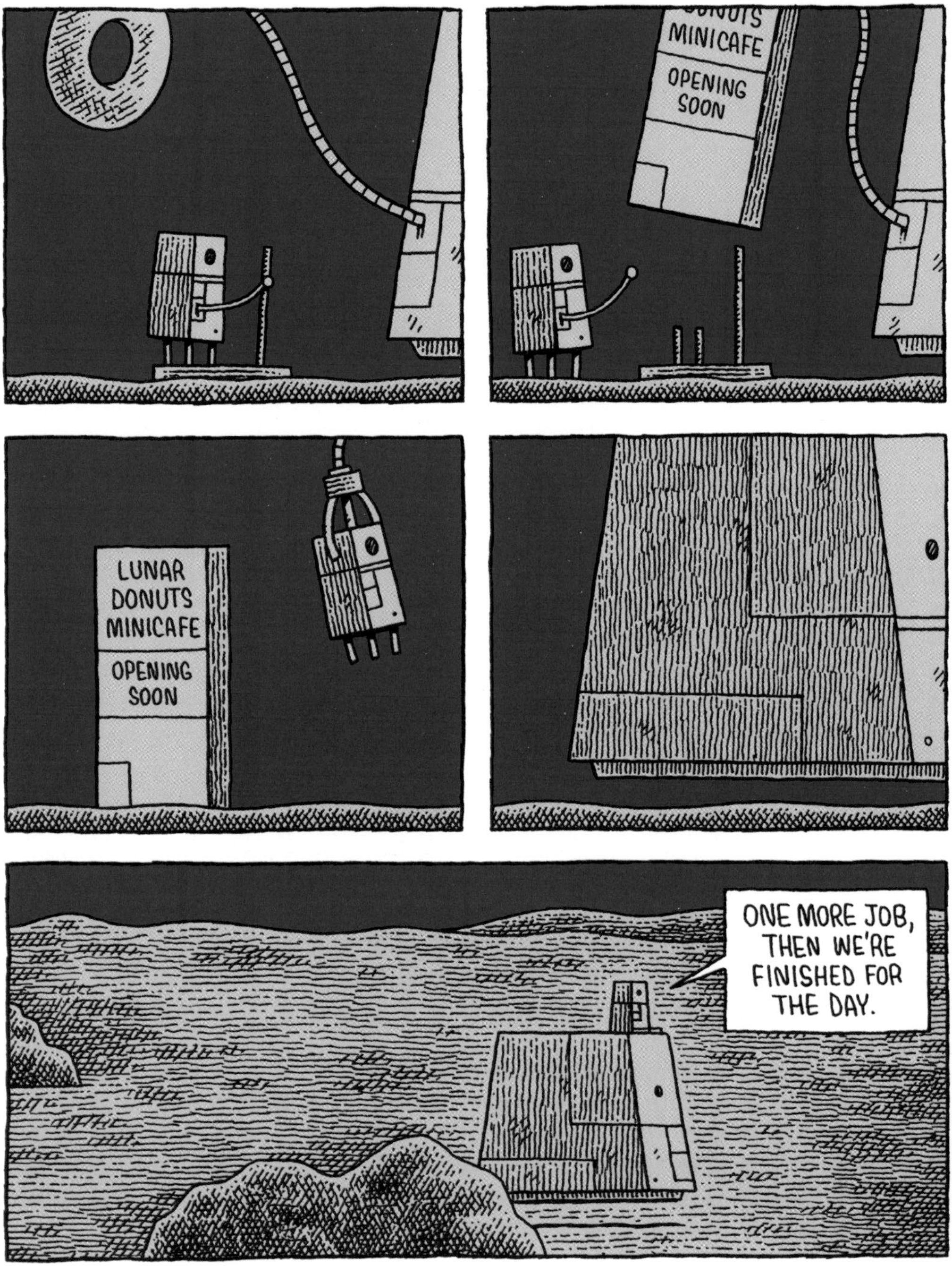
DONUTS
MINICAFE
OPENING
SOON
LUNAR
DONUTS
MINICAFE
OPENING
SOON
ONE MORE JOB, THEN WE'RE FINISHED FOR THE DAY.

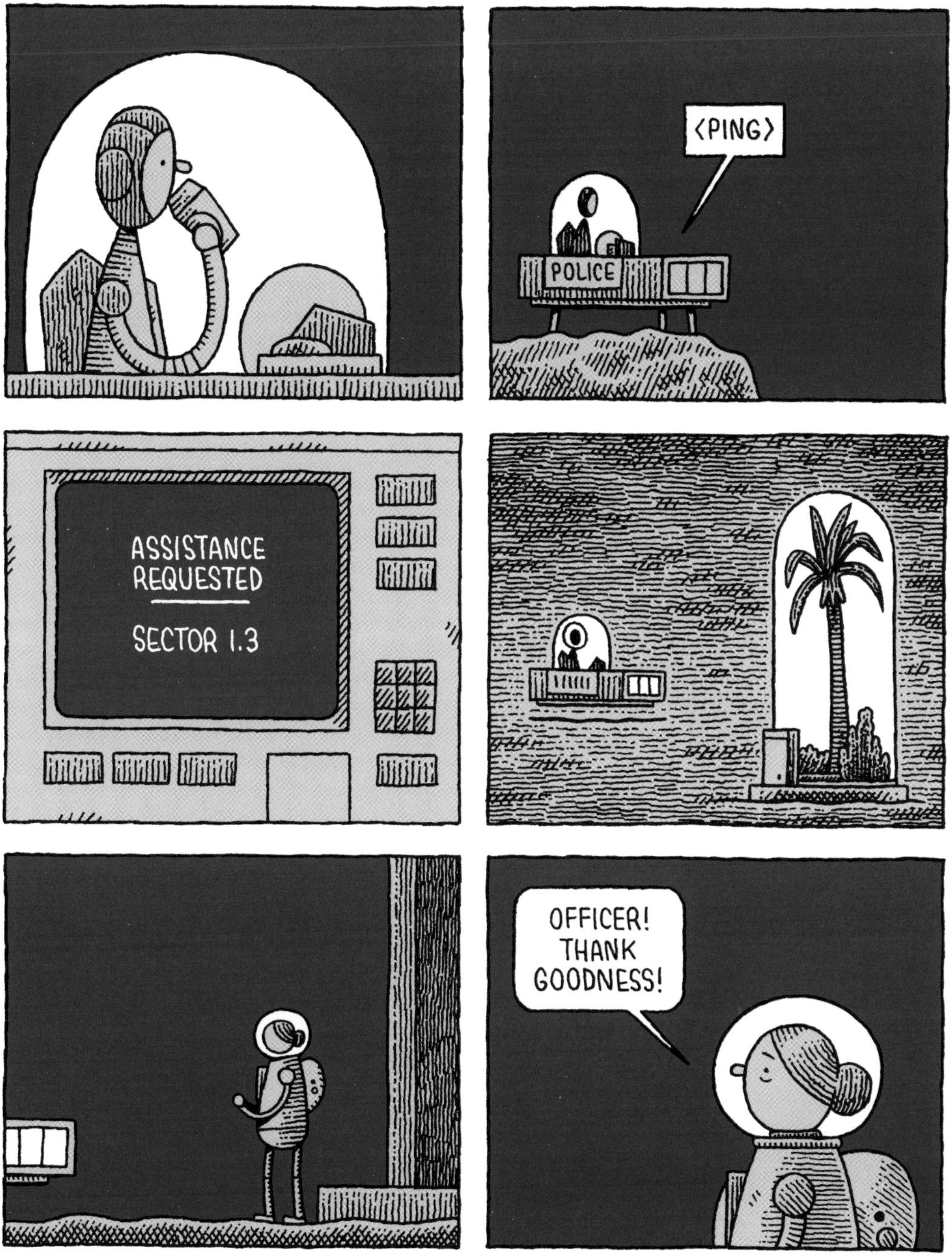
<PING>
POLICE
ASSISTANCE REQUESTED
SECTOR 1.3
OFFICER! THANK GOODNESS!

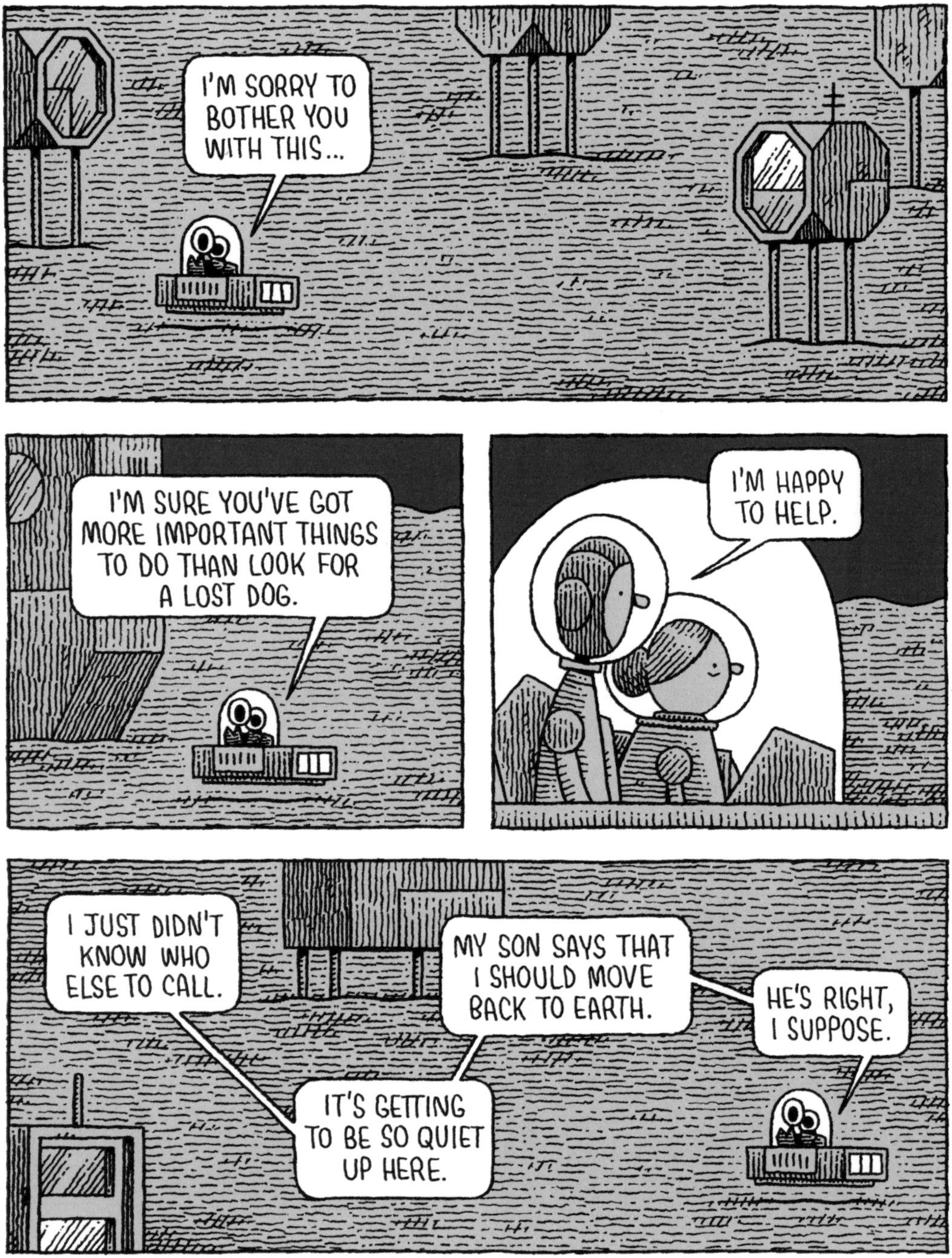

I'M SORRY TO BOTHER YOU WITH THIS...
I'M SURE YOU'VE GOT MORE IMPORTANT THINGS TO DO THAN LOOK FOR A LOST DOG.
I'M HAPPY TO HELP.
I JUST DIDN'T KNOW WHO ELSE TO CALL.
IT'S GETTING TO BE SO QUIET UP HERE.
MY SON SAYS THAT I SHOULD MOVE BACK TO EARTH.
HE'S RIGHT, I SUPPOSE.

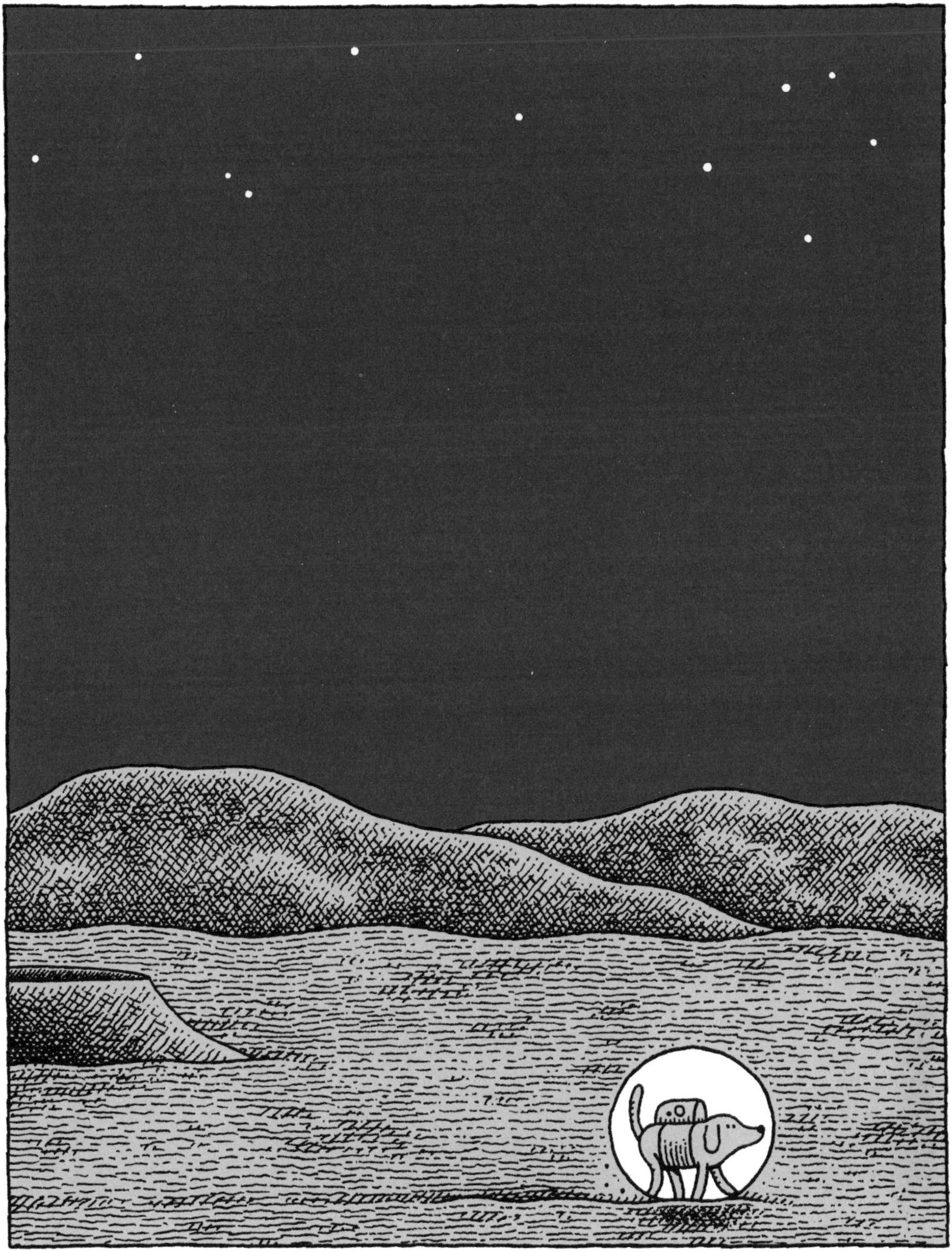

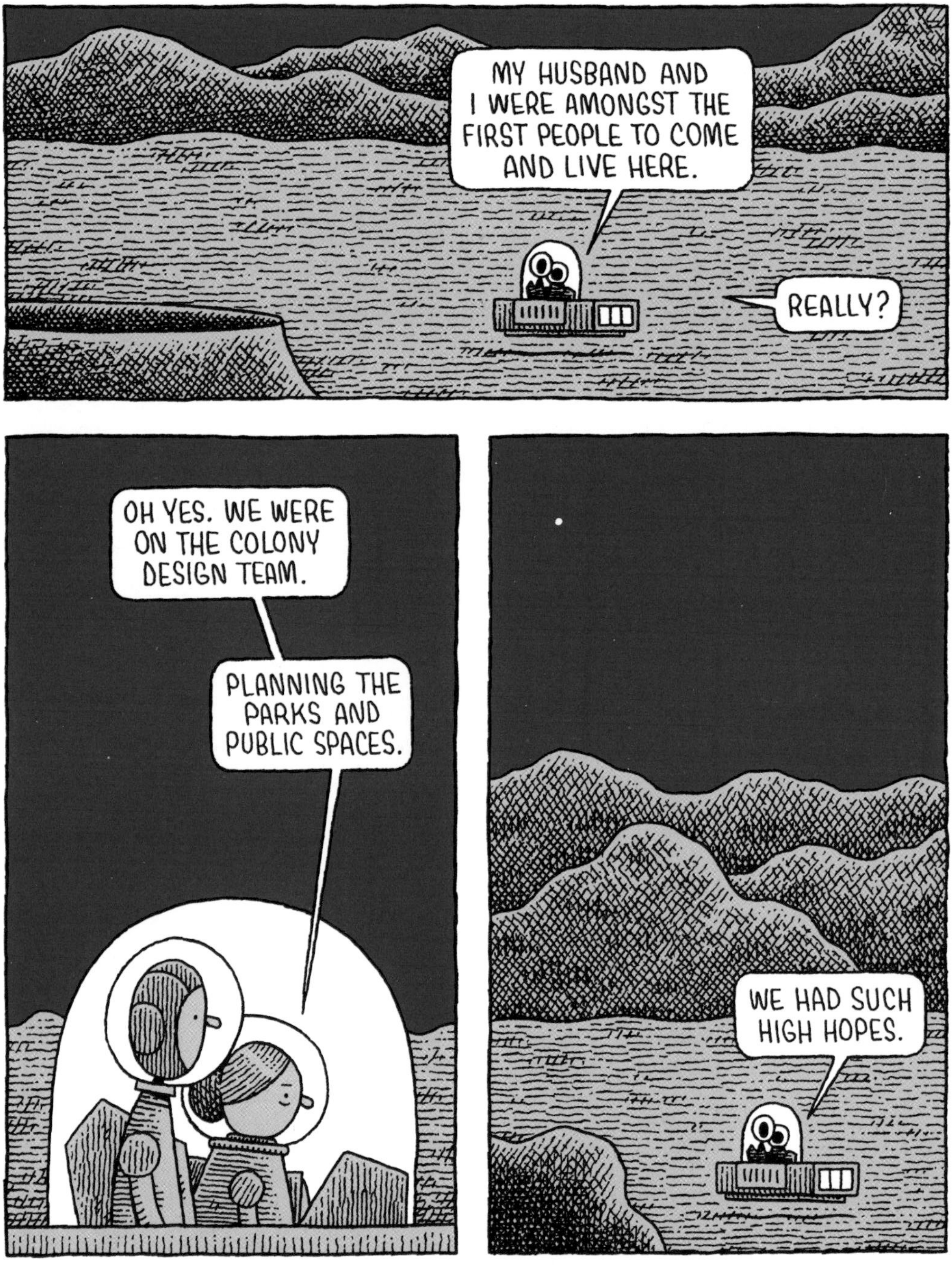
MY HUSBAND AND I WERE AMONGST THE FIRST PEOPLE TO COME AND LIVE HERE.
REALLY?
OH YES. WE WERE ON THE COLONY DESIGN TEAM.
PLANNING THE PARKS AND PUBLIC SPACES.
WE HAD SUCH HIGH HOPES.

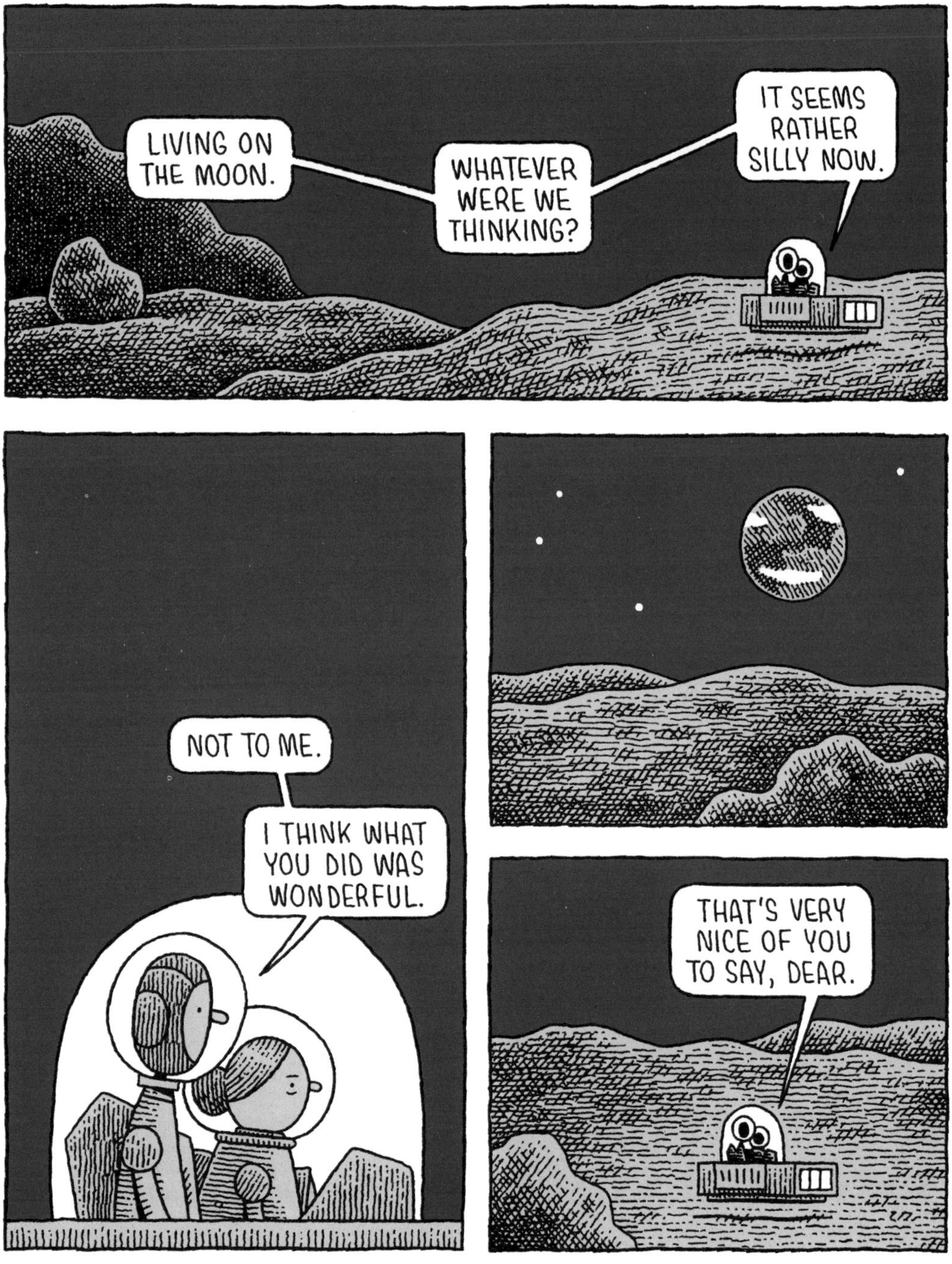
LIVING ON THE MOON.
WHATEVER WERE WE THINKING?
IT SEEMS RATHER SILLY NOW.
NOT TO ME.
I THINK WHAT YOU DID WAS WONDERFUL.
THAT'S VERY NICE OF YOU TO SAY, DEAR.

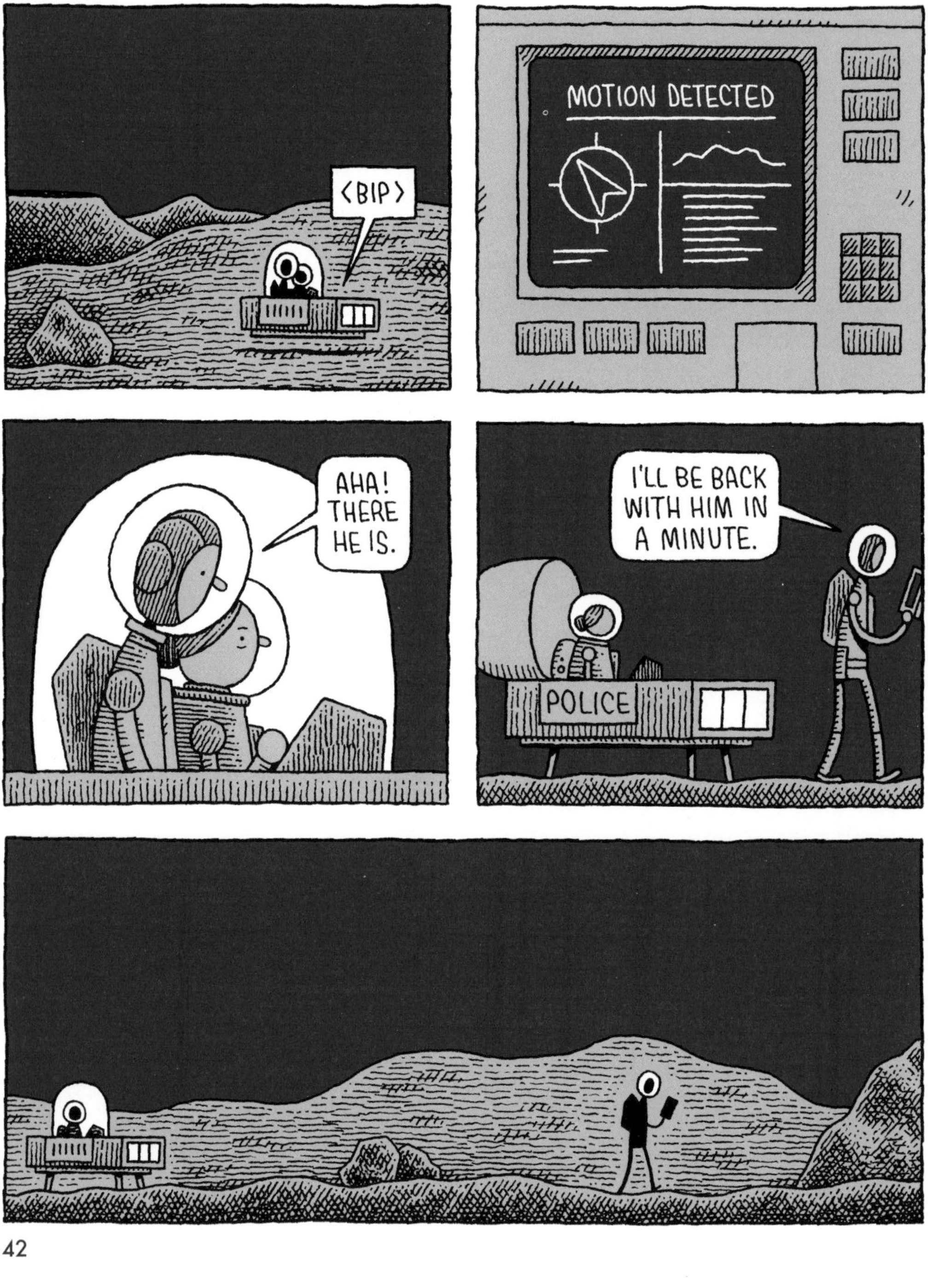

<BIP>
MOTION DETECTED
AHA! THERE HE IS.
I'LL BE BACK WITH HIM IN A MINUTE.
POLICE

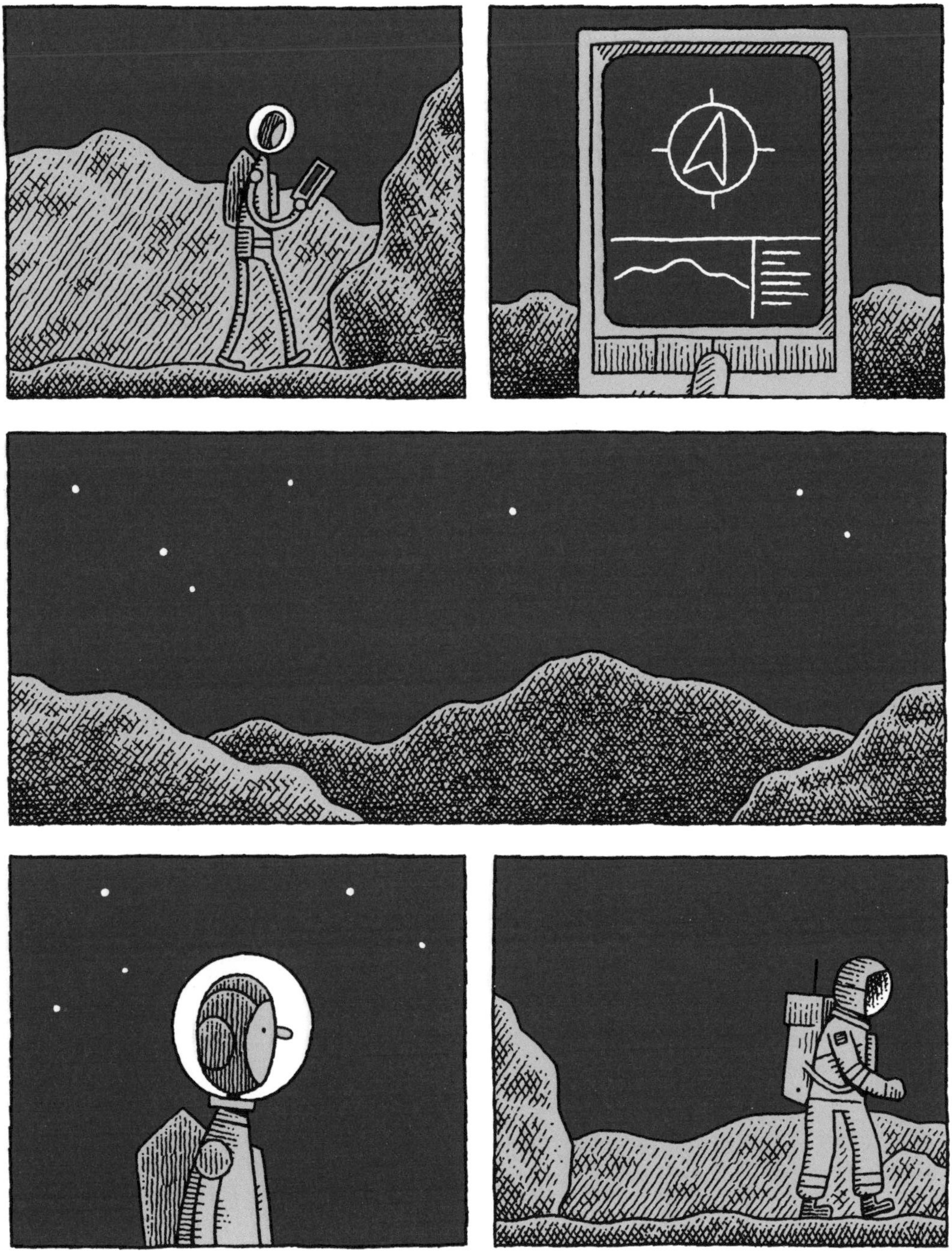

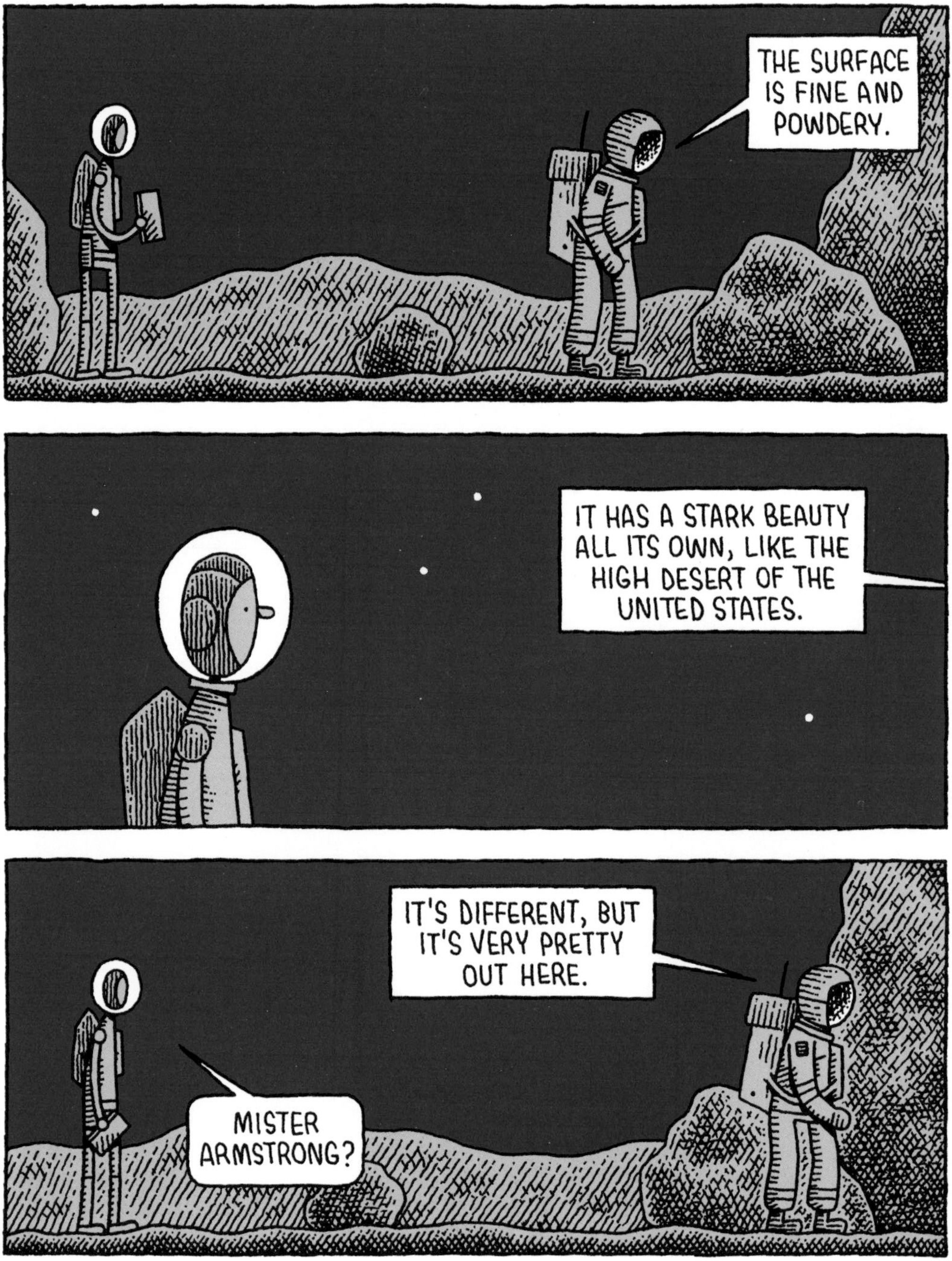
THE SURFACE IS FINE AND POWDERY.
IT HAS A STARK BEAUTY ALL ITS OWN, LIKE THE HIGH DESERT OF THE UNITED STATES.
IT'S DIFFERENT, BUT IT'S VERY PRETTY OUT HERE.
MISTER ARMSTRONG?

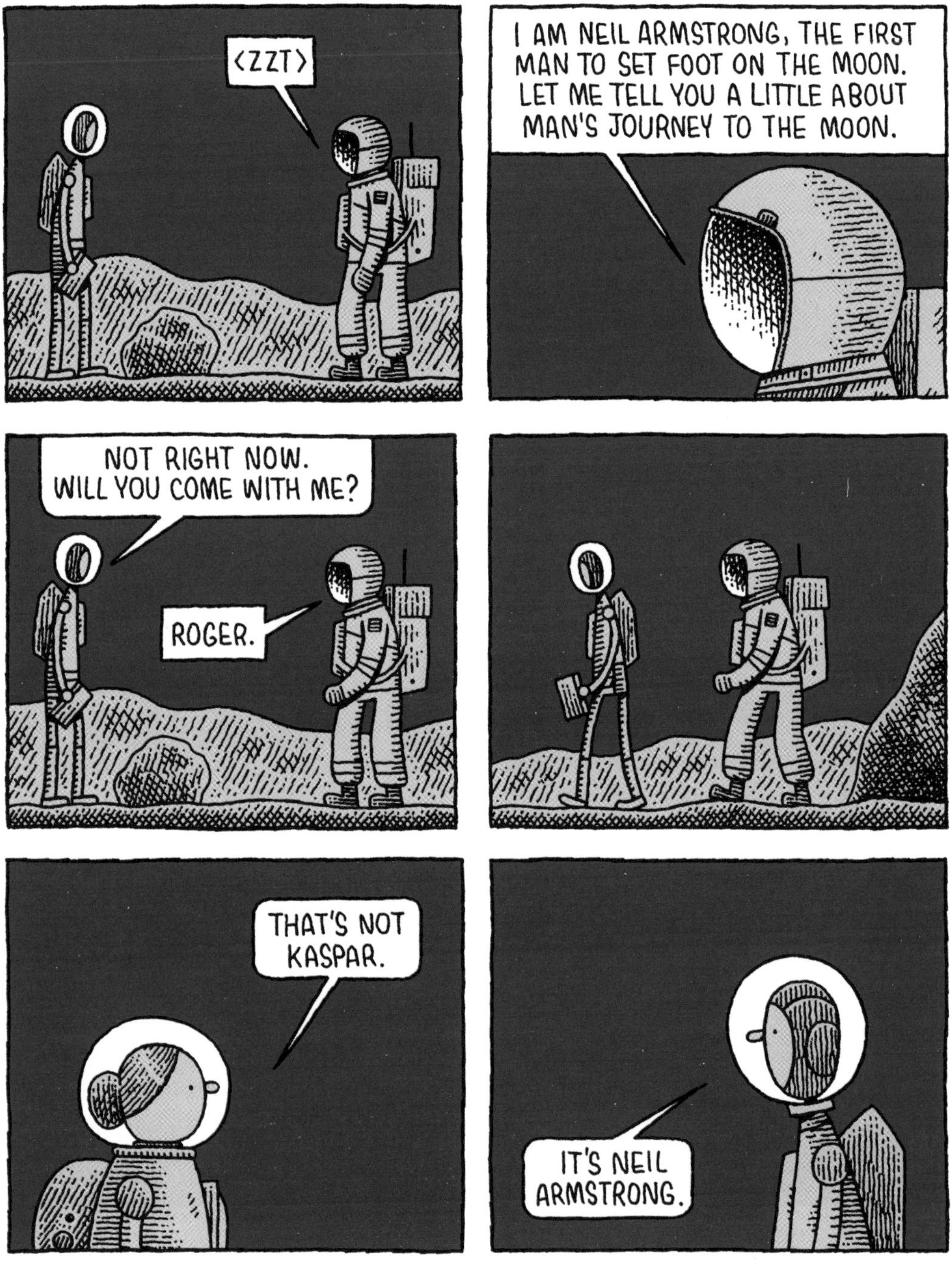
<ZZT>
I AM NEIL ARMSTRONG, THE FIRST MAN TO SET FOOT ON THE MOON. LET ME TELL YOU A LITTLE ABOUT MAN'S JOURNEY TO THE MOON.
NOT RIGHT NOW. WILL YOU COME WITH ME?
ROGER.
THAT'S NOT KASPAR.
IT'S NEIL ARMSTRONG.

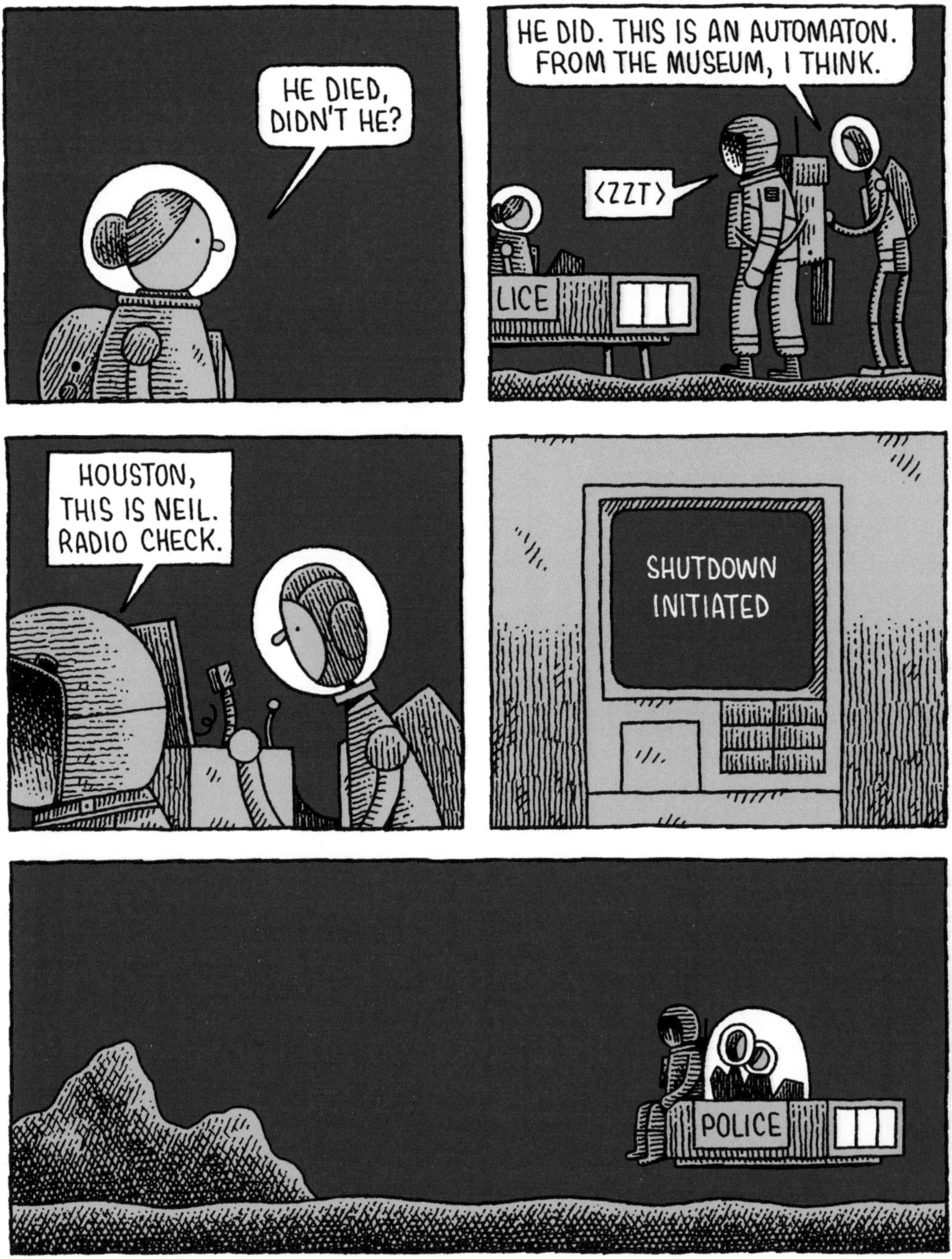
HE DIED, DIDN'T HE?
HE DID. THIS IS AN AUTOMATON. FROM THE MUSEUM, I THINK.
<ZZT>
LICE
HOUSTON, THIS IS NEIL. RADIO CHECK.
SHUTDOWN INITIATED
POLICE

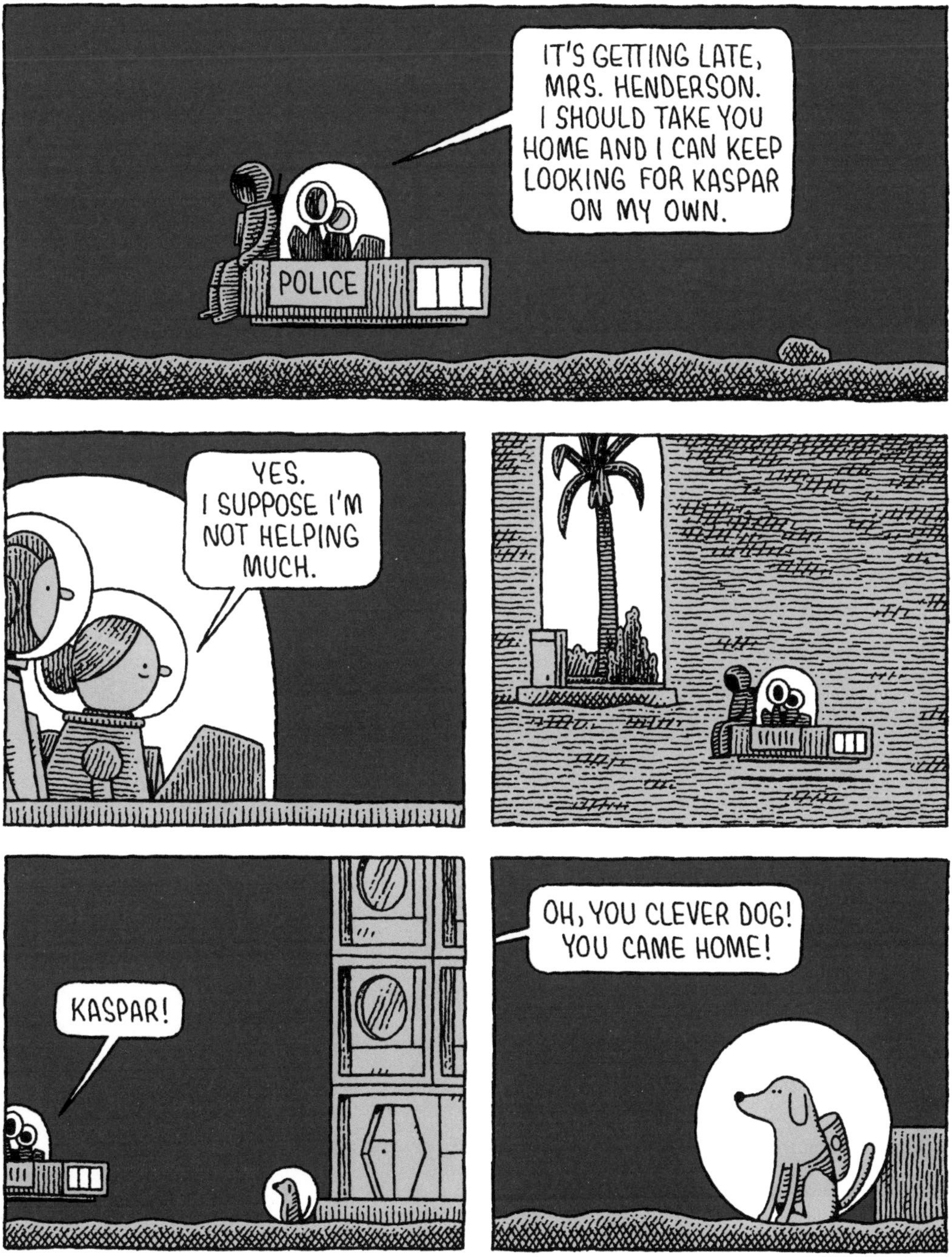
IT'S GETTING LATE, MRS. HENDERSON. I SHOULD TAKE YOU HOME AND I CAN KEEP LOOKING FOR KASPAR ON MY OWN.
POLICE
YES. I SUPPOSE I'M NOT HELPING MUCH.
KASPAR!
OH, YOU CLEVER DOG! YOU CAME HOME!

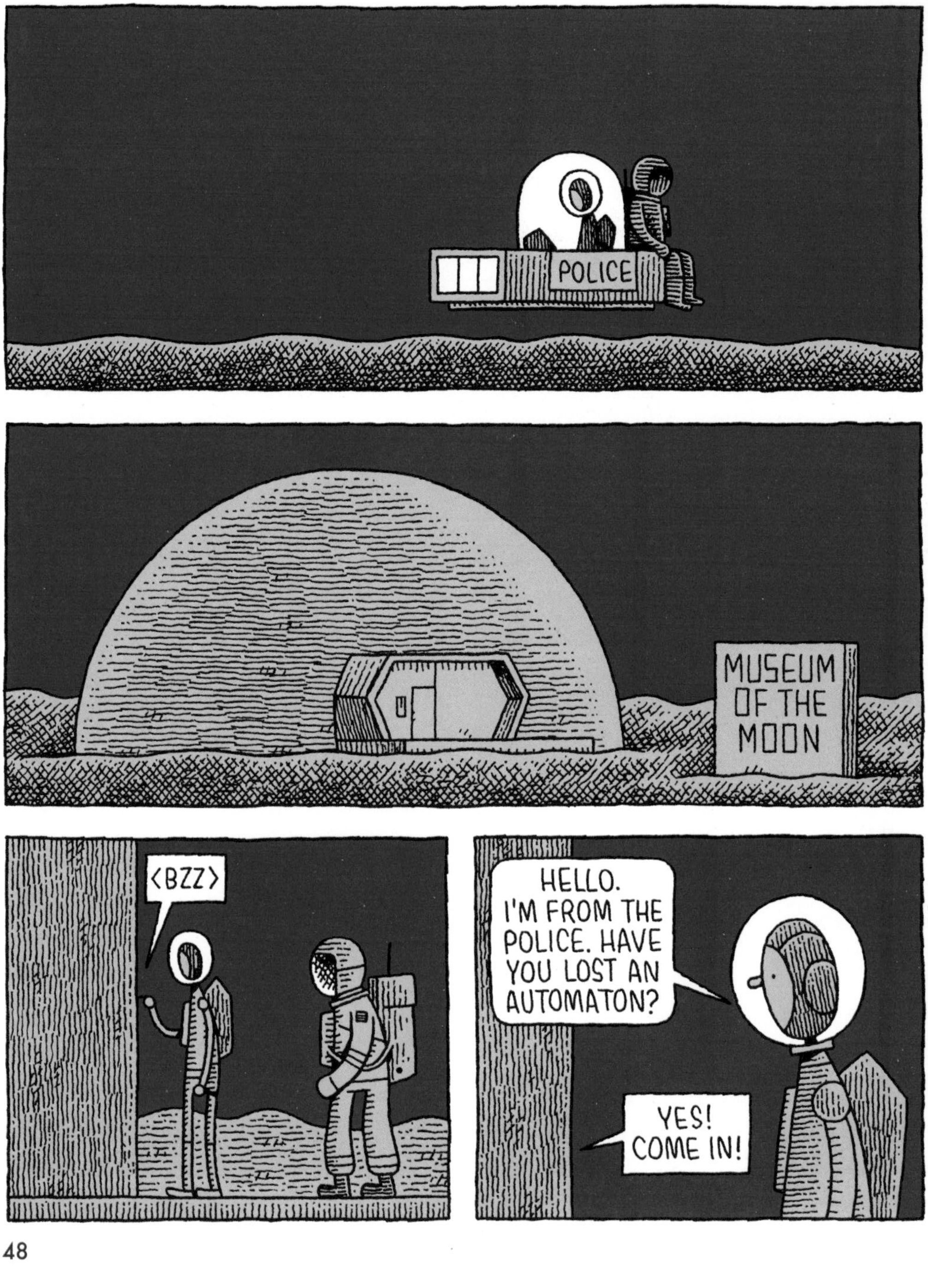
POLICE
MUSEUM OF THE MOON
<BZZ>
HELLO. I'M FROM THE POLICE. HAVE YOU LOST AN AUTOMATON?
YES! COME IN!

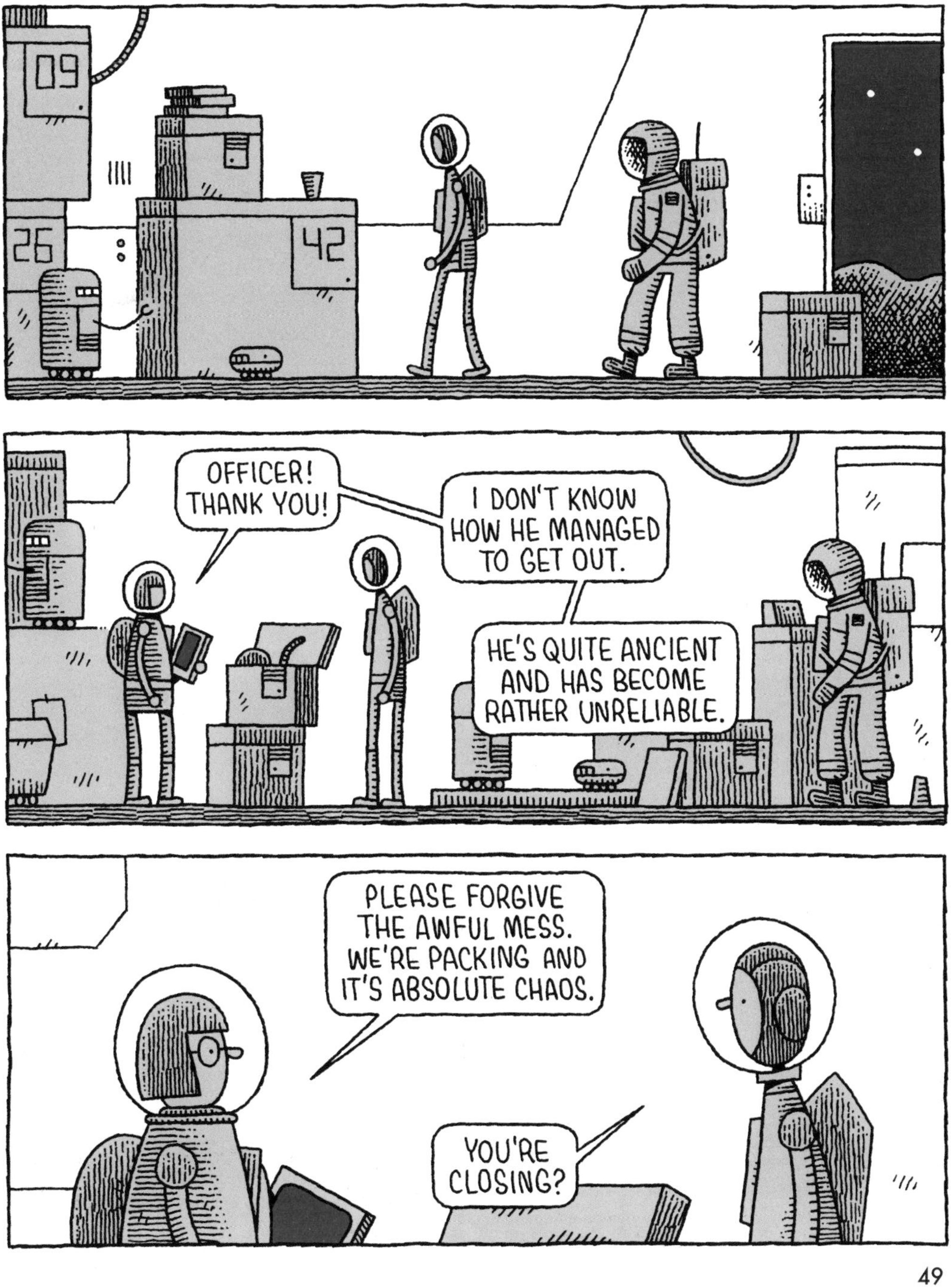
09
26
42
OFFICER! THANK YOU!
I DON'T KNOW HOW HE MANAGED TO GET OUT.
HE'S QUITE ANCIENT AND HAS BECOME RATHER UNRELIABLE.
PLEASE FORGIVE THE AWFUL MESS. WE'RE PACKING AND IT'S ABSOLUTE CHAOS.
YOU'RE CLOSING?

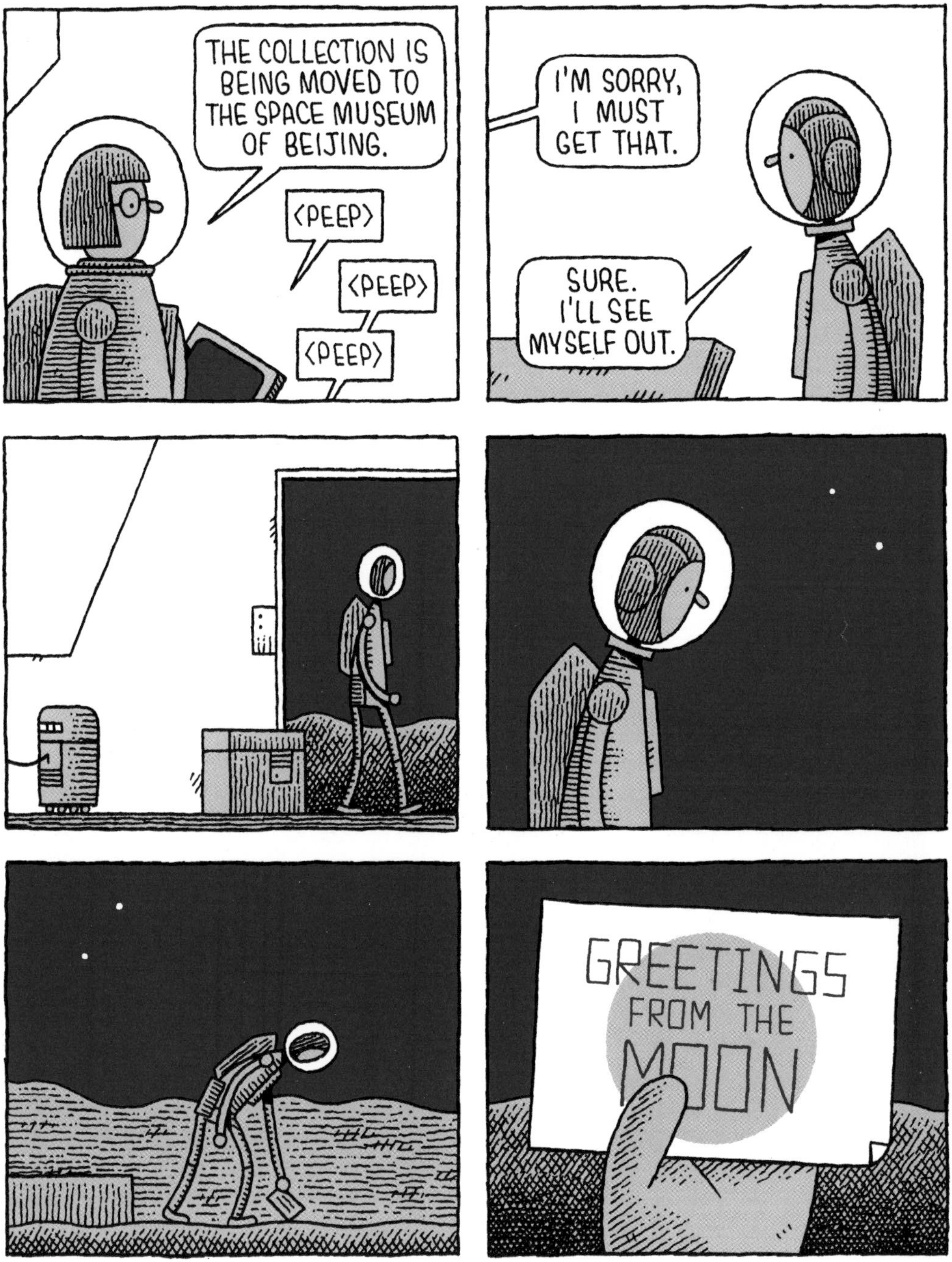
THE COLLECTION IS BEING MOVED TO THE SPACE MUSEUM OF BEIJING.
<PEEP>
<PEEP>
<PEEP>
I'M SORRY, I MUST GET THAT.
SURE. I'LL SEE MYSELF OUT.
GREETINGS FROM THE MOON

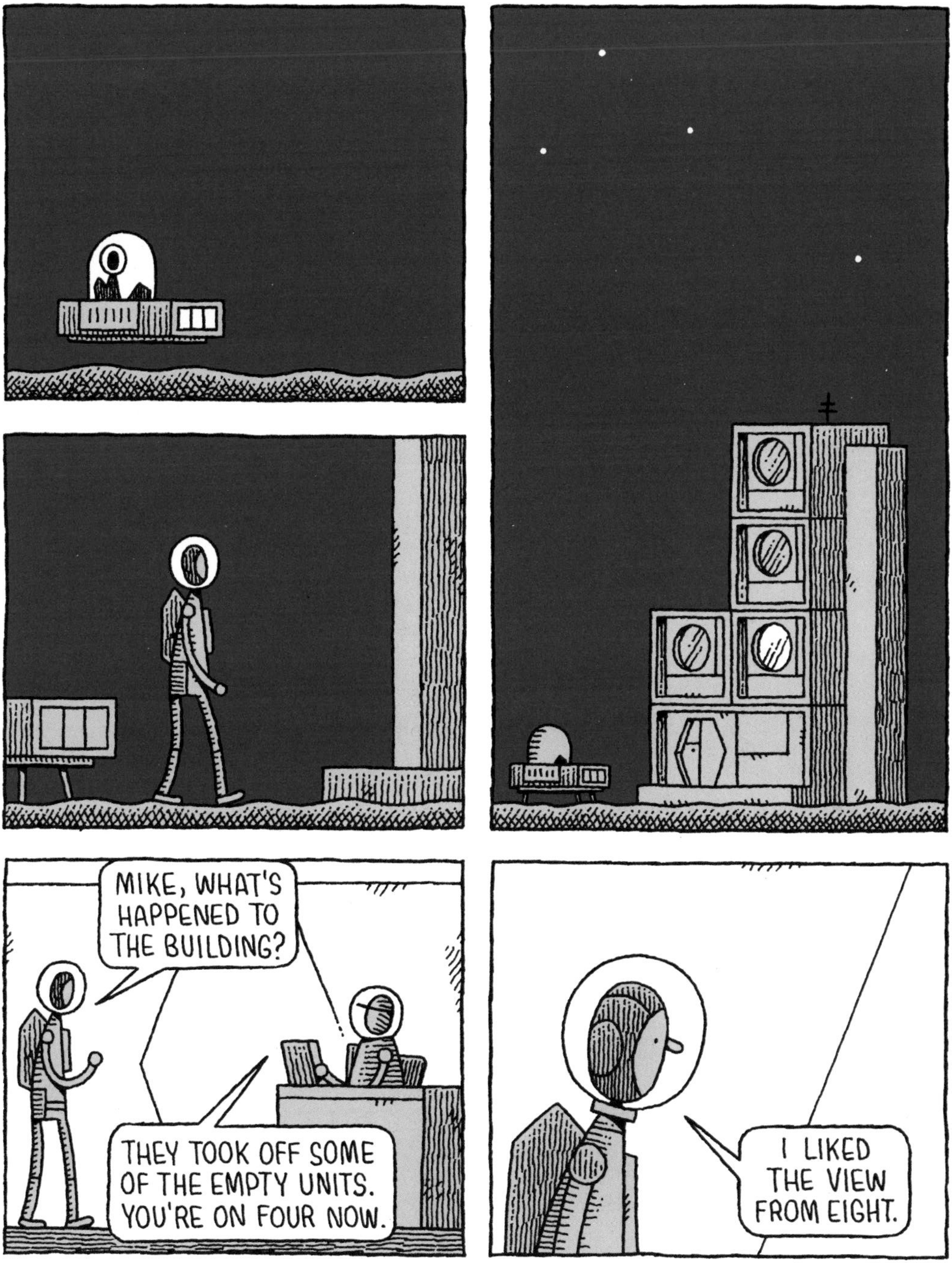
MIKE, WHAT'S HAPPENED TO THE BUILDING?
THEY TOOK OFF SOME OF THE EMPTY UNITS. YOU'RE ON FOUR NOW.
I LIKED THE VIEW FROM EIGHT.

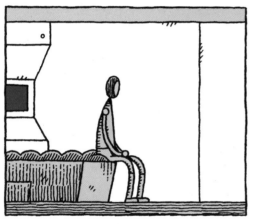

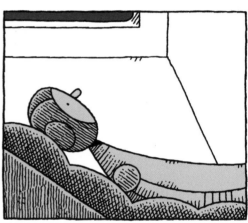

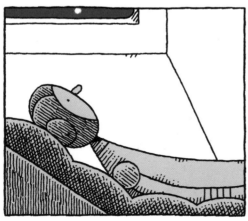

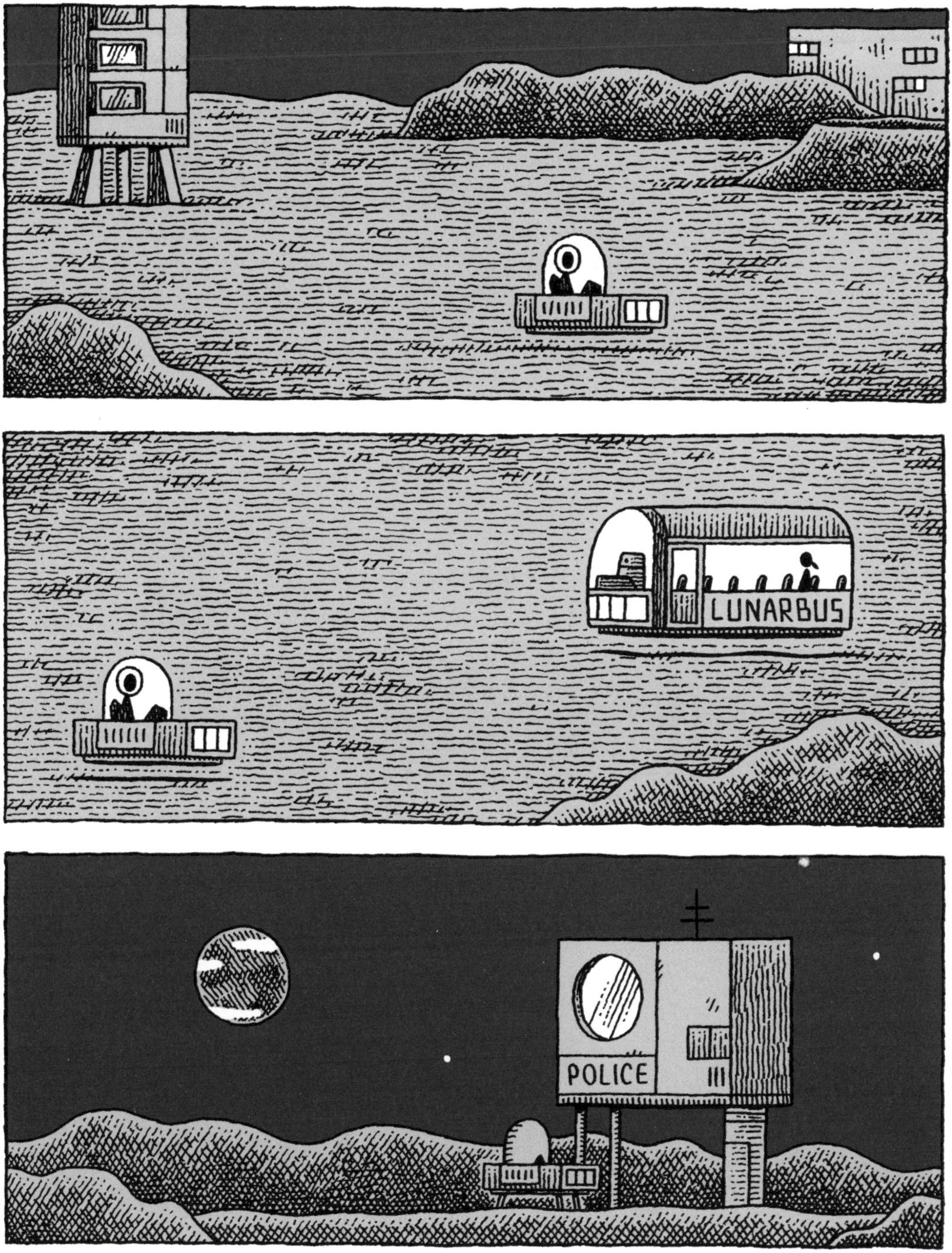
LUNARBUS
POLICE

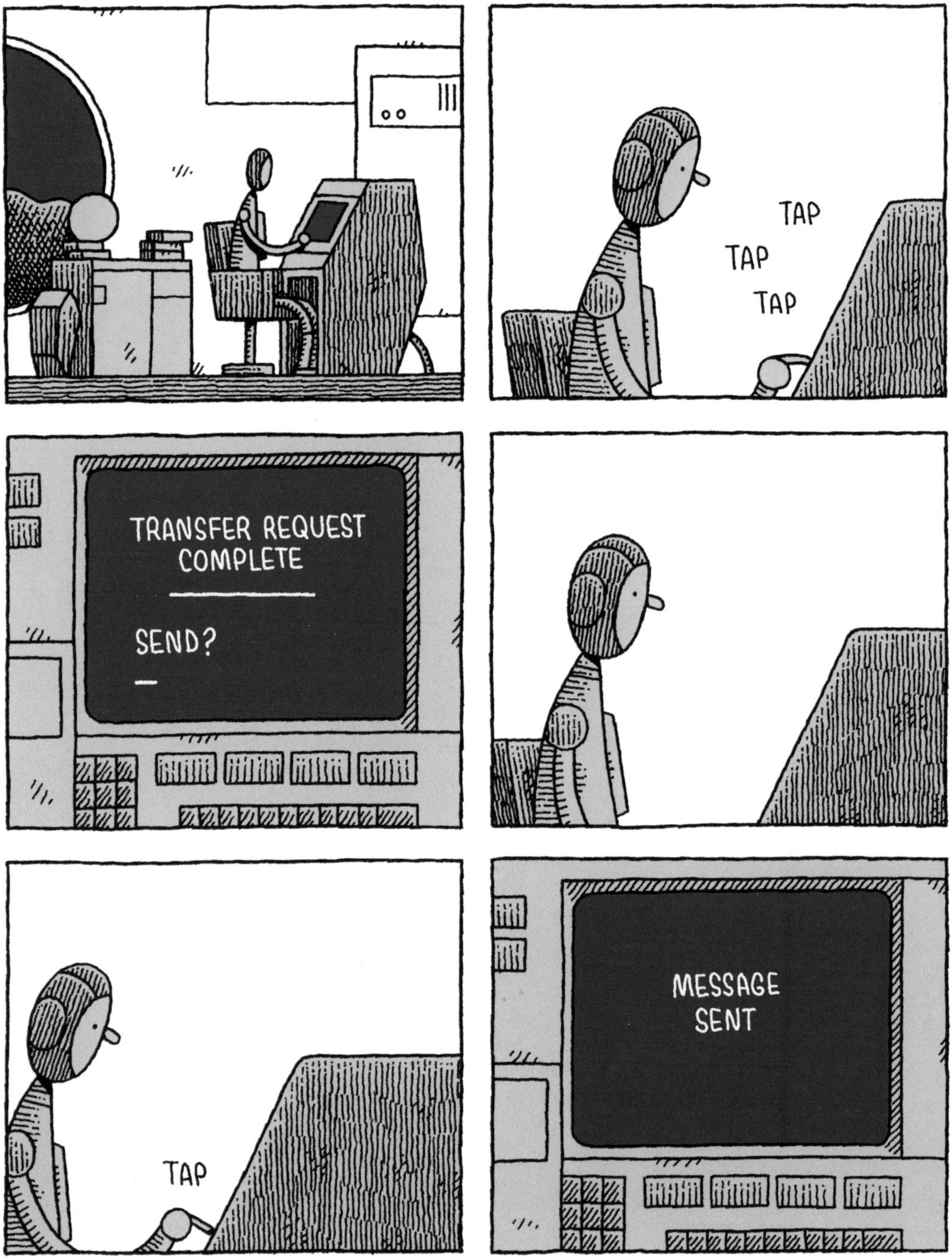
TAP
TAP
TAP
TRANSFER REQUEST
COMPLETE
SEND?
TAP
MESSAGE
SENT

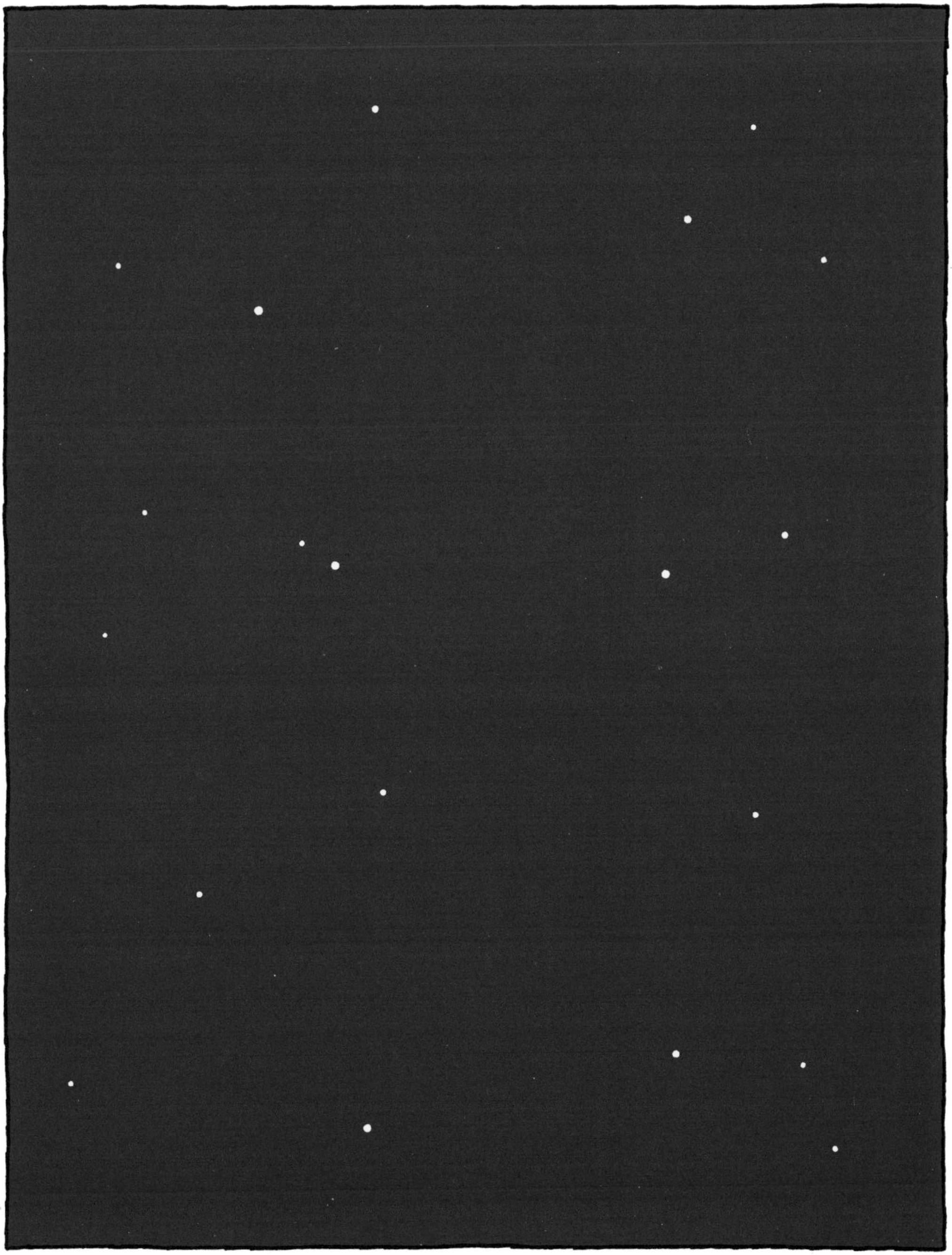

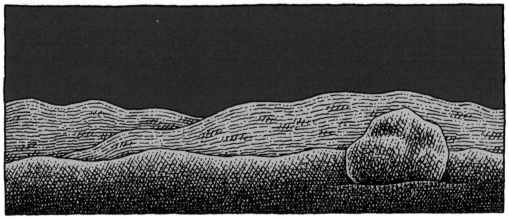

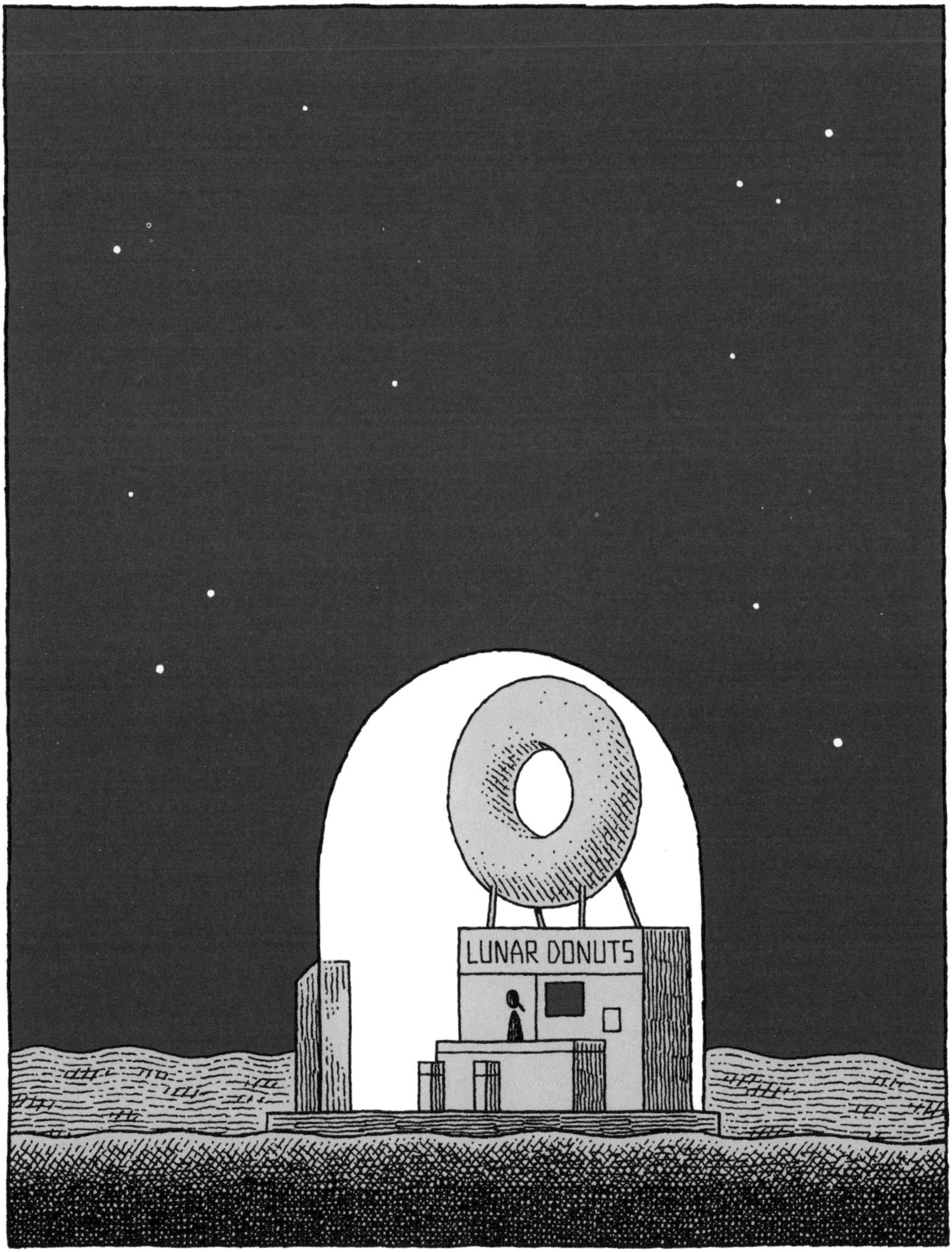
LUNAR DONUTS

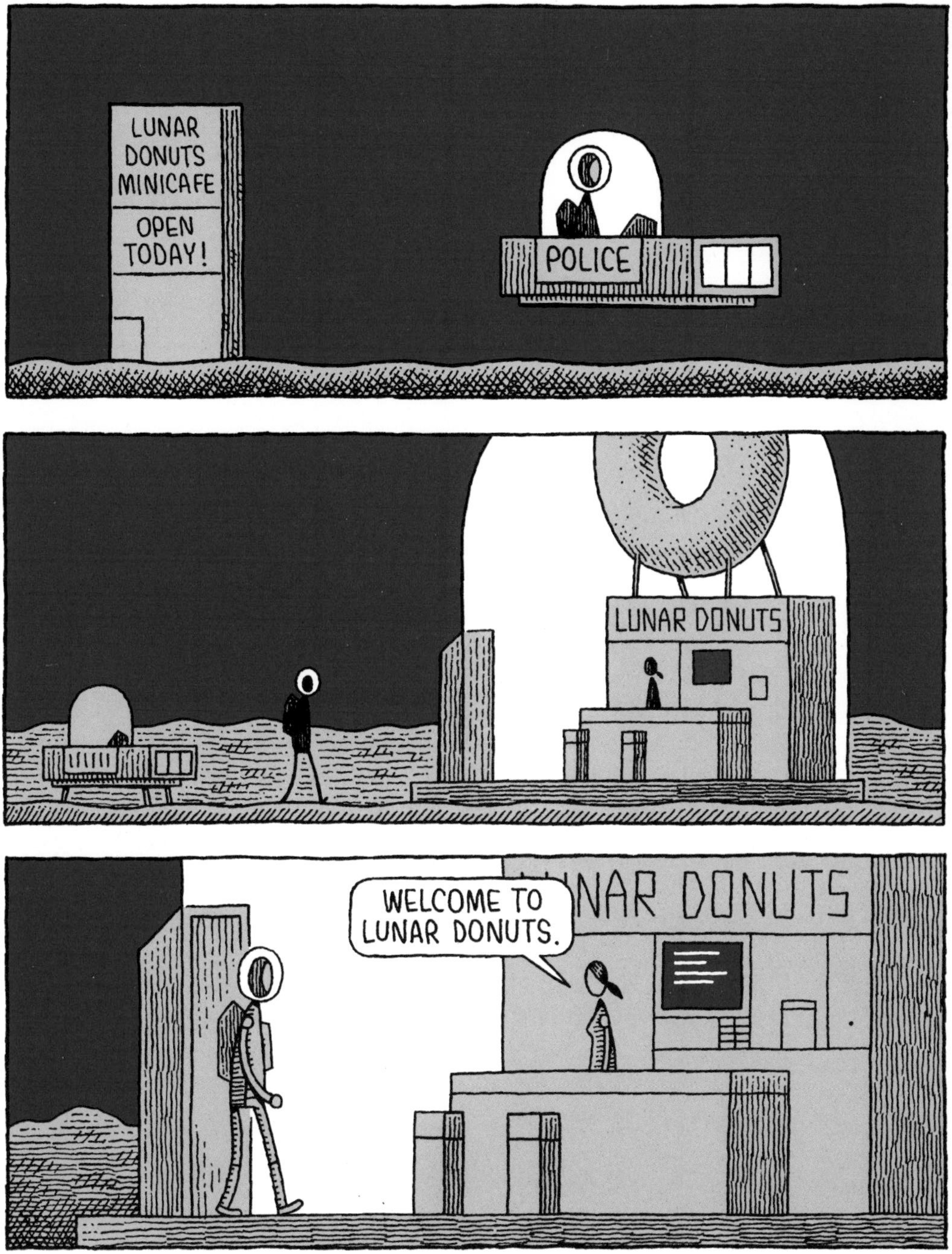
LUNAR
DONUTS
MINICAFE
OPEN
TODAY!
POLICE
LUNAR DONUTS
WELCOME TO
LUNAR DONUTS.

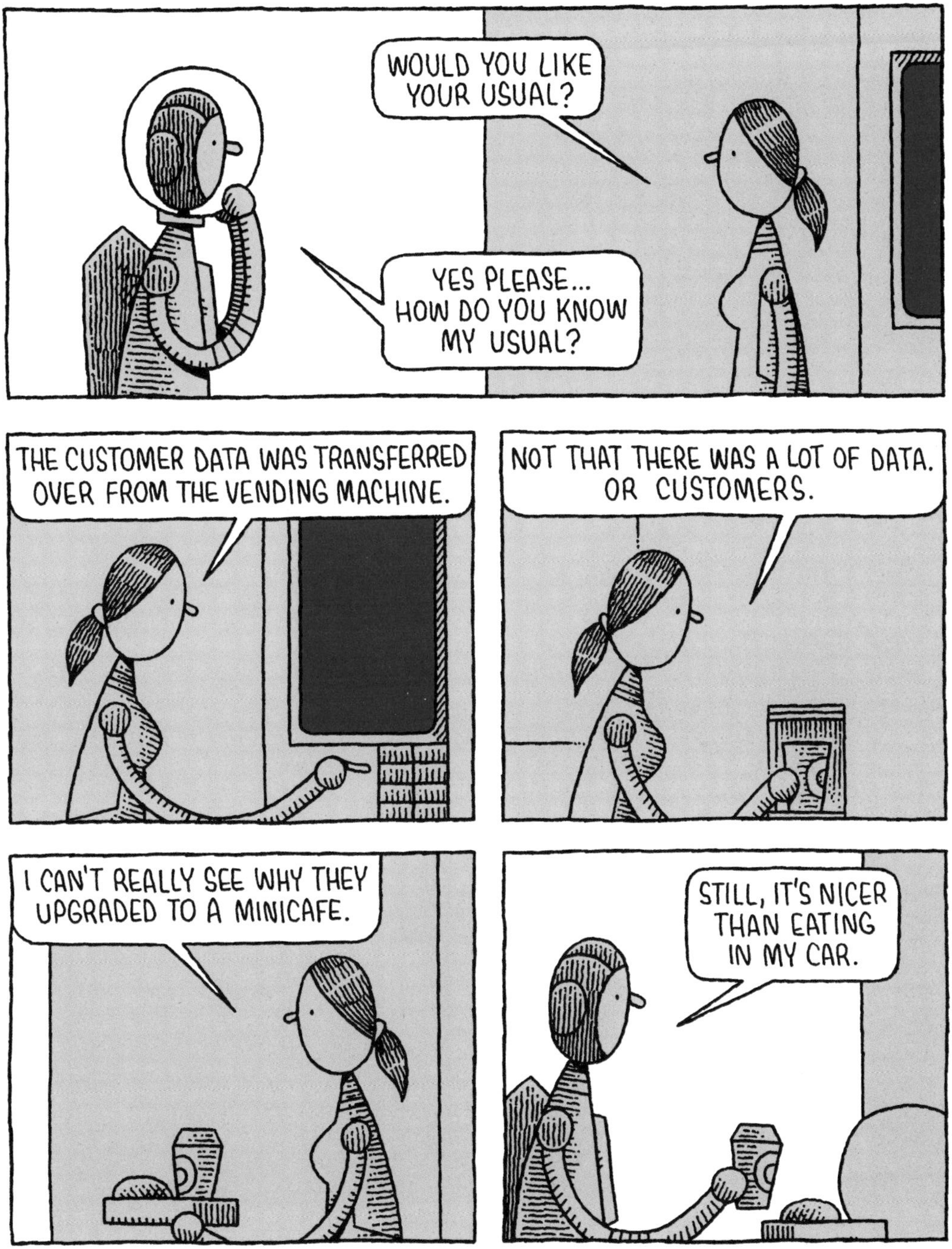
WOULD YOU LIKE YOUR USUAL?
YES PLEASE... HOW DO YOU KNOW MY USUAL?
THE CUSTOMER DATA WAS TRANSFERRED OVER FROM THE VENDING MACHINE.
NOT THAT THERE WAS A LOT OF DATA. OR CUSTOMERS.
I CAN'T REALLY SEE WHY THEY UPGRADED TO A MINICAFE.
STILL, IT'S NICER THAN EATING IN MY CAR.

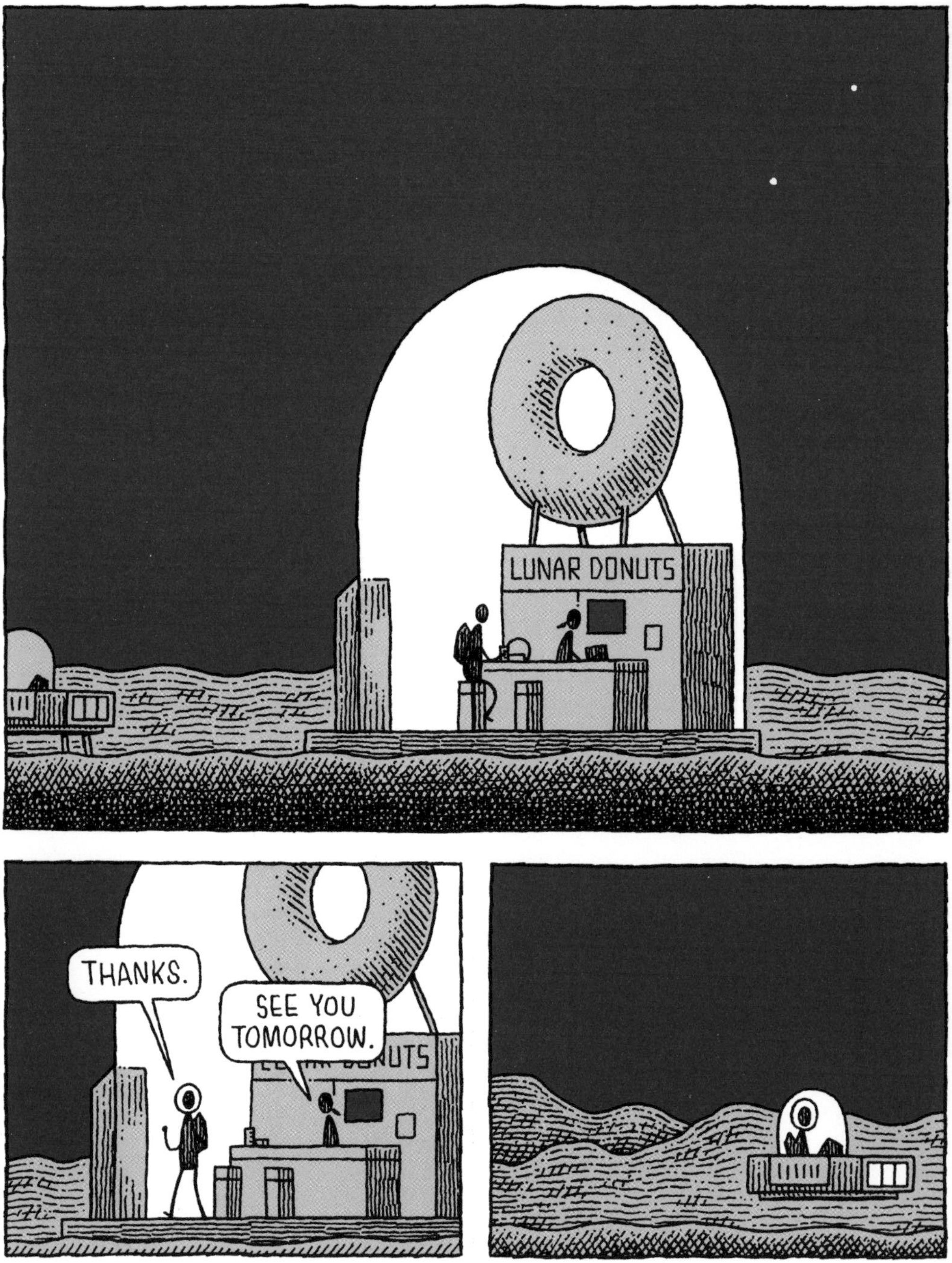
LUNAR DONUTS
THANKS.
SEE YOU TOMORROW.

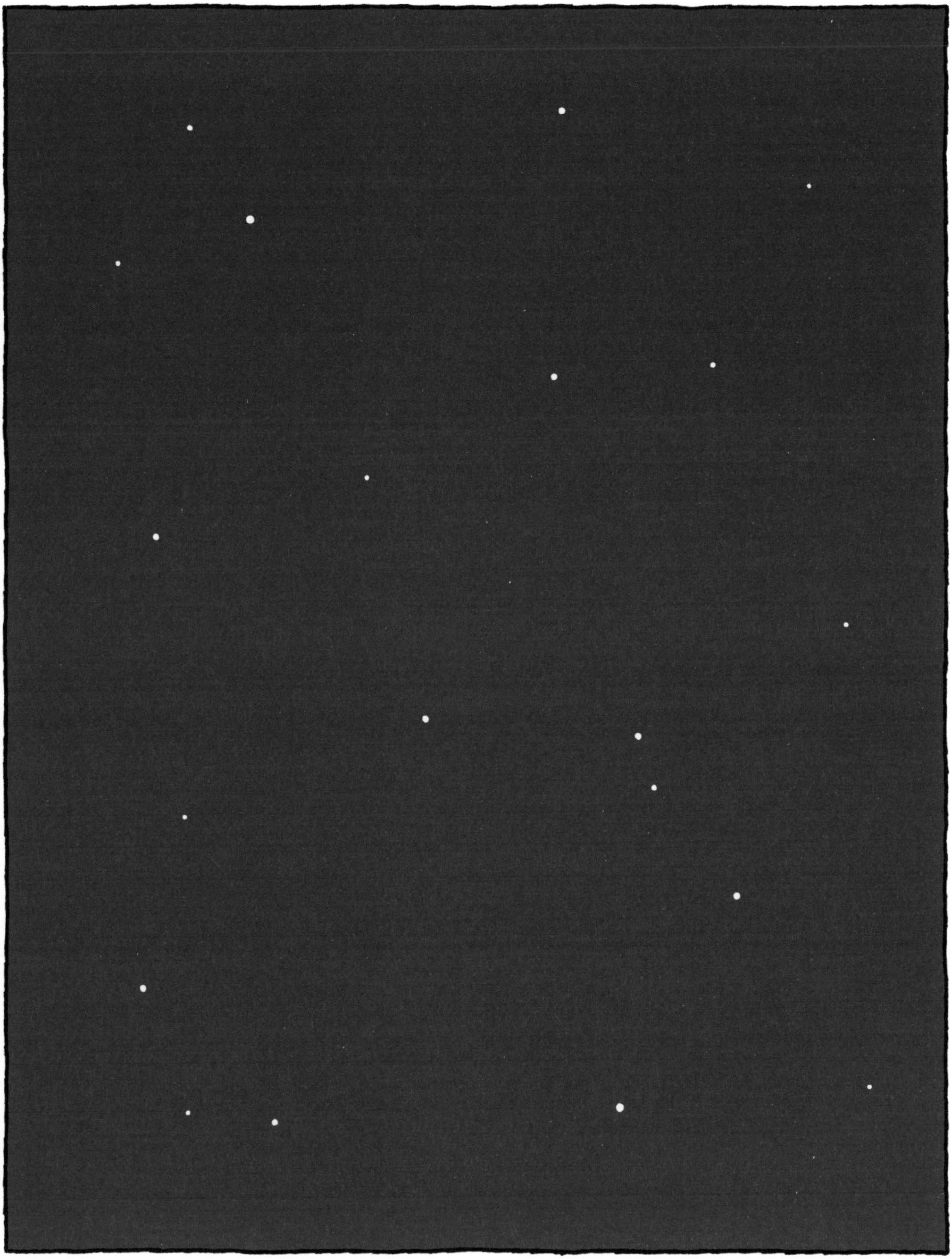

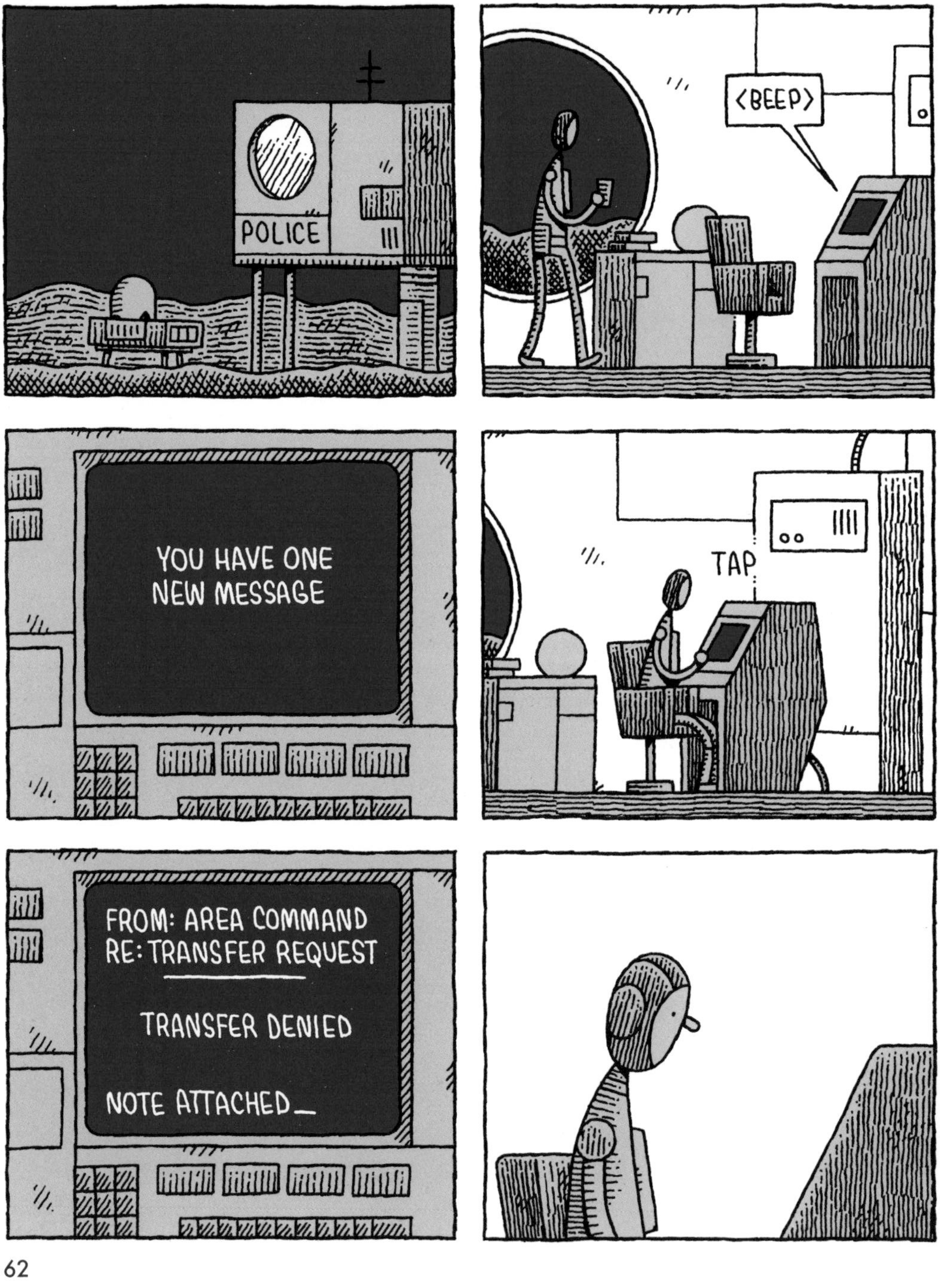
POLICE
<BEEP>
YOU HAVE ONE NEW MESSAGE
TAP
FROM: AREA COMMAND
RE: TRANSFER REQUEST
TRANSFER DENIED
NOTE ATTACHED_

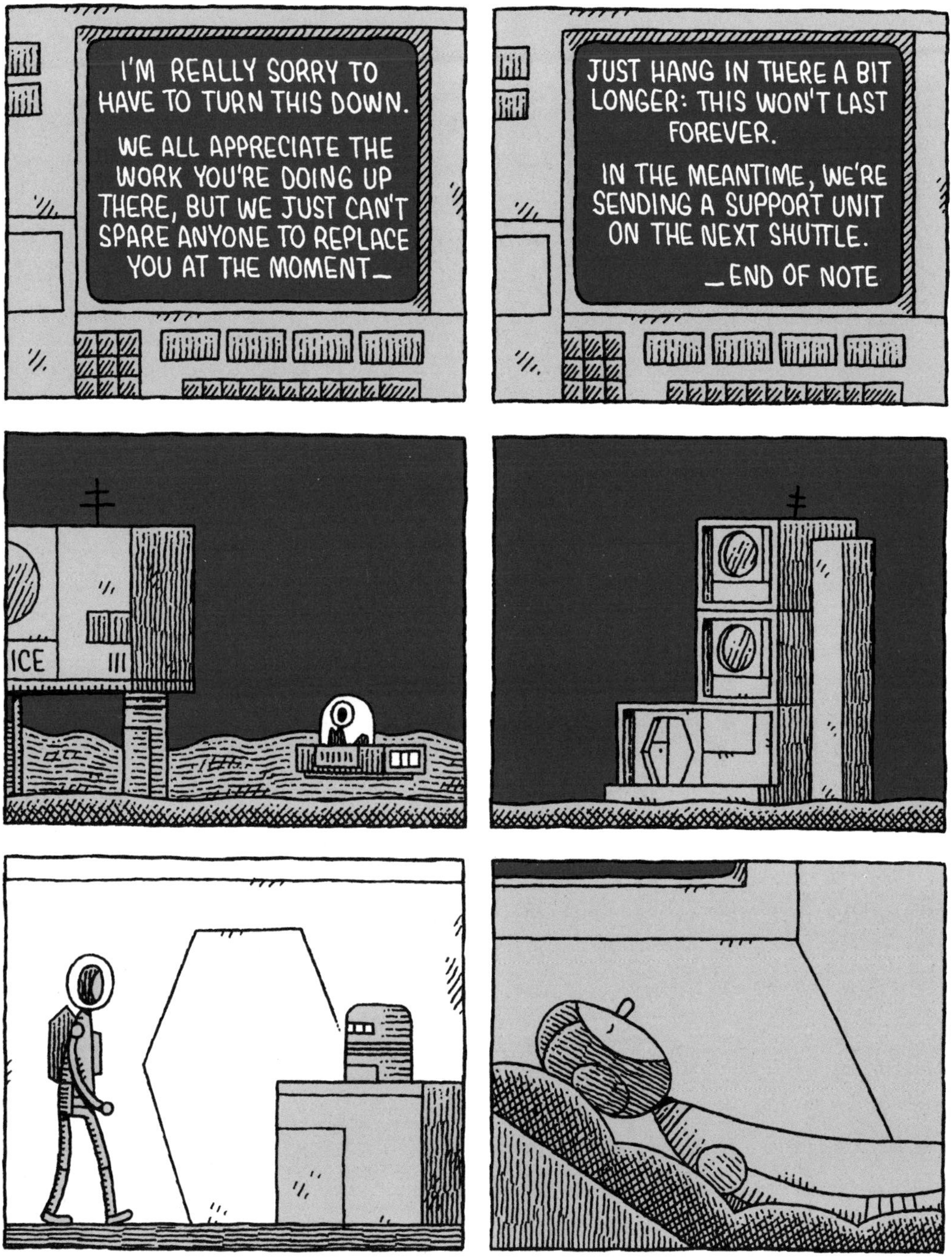
I'M REALLY SORRY TO HAVE TO TURN THIS DOWN.
WE ALL APPRECIATE THE WORK YOU'RE DOING UP THERE, BUT WE JUST CAN'T SPARE ANYONE TO REPLACE YOU AT THE MOMENT_
JUST HANG IN THERE A BIT LONGER: THIS WON'T LAST FOREVER.
IN THE MEANTIME, WE'RE SENDING A SUPPORT UNIT ON THE NEXT SHUTTLE.
_END OF NOTE
ICE

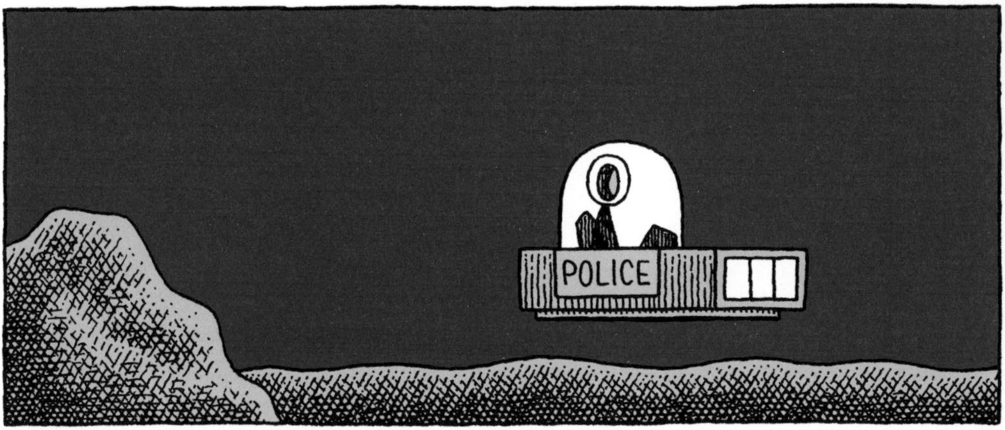
POLICE

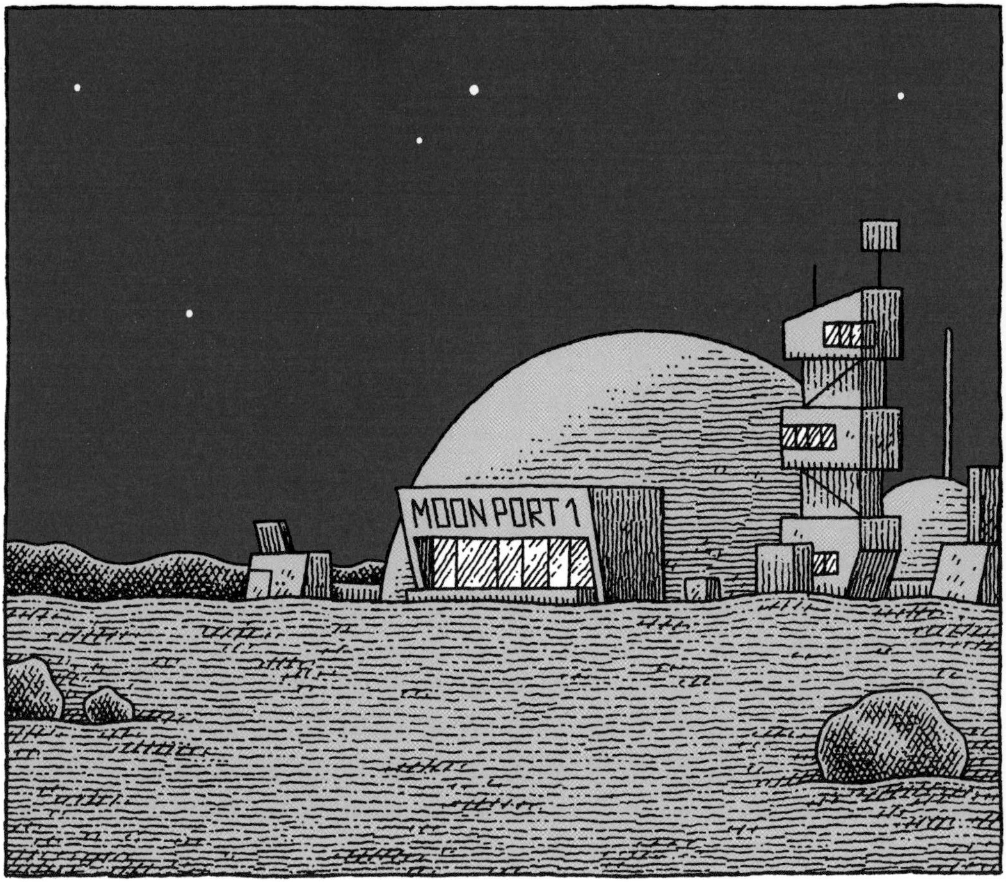
MOON PORT 1

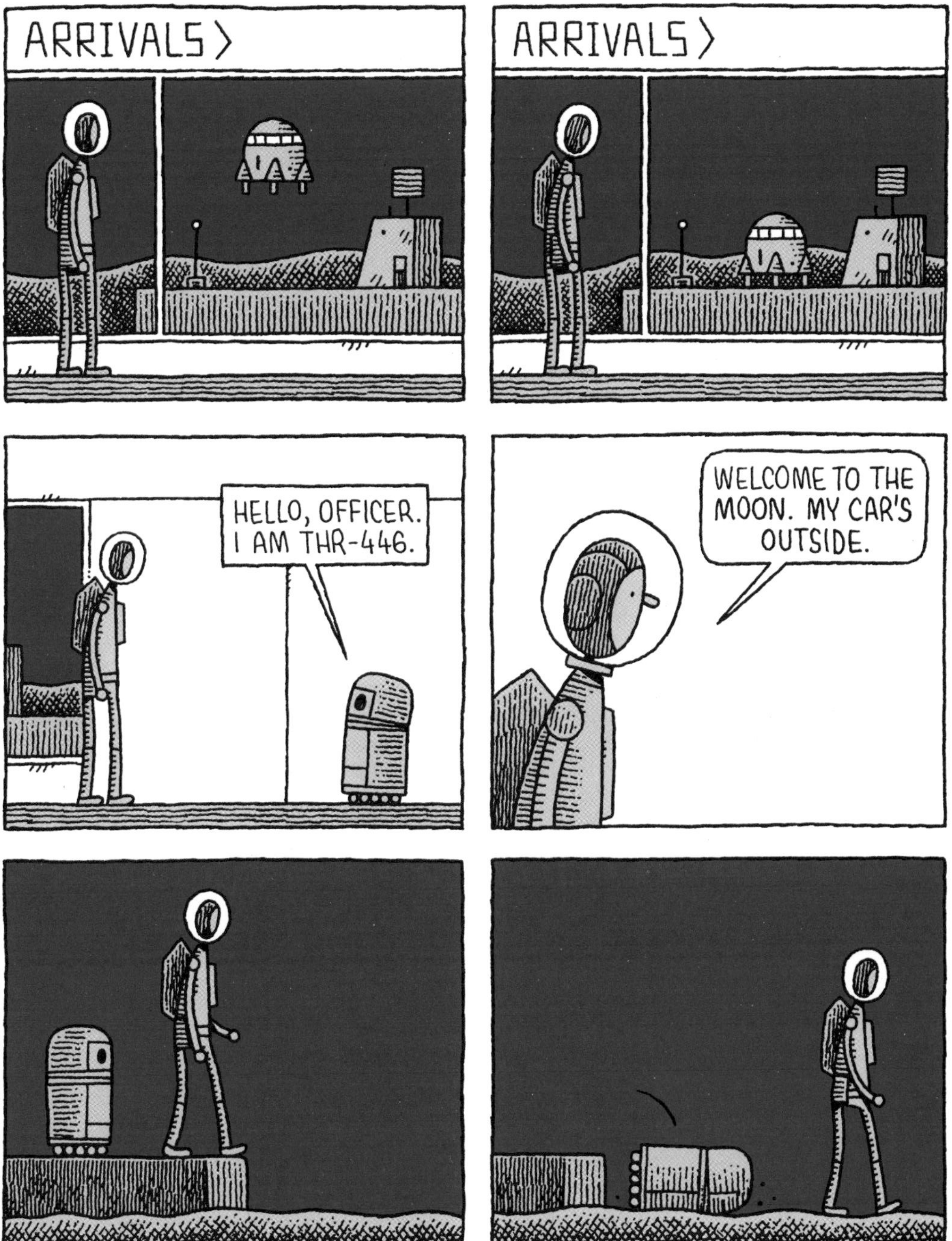
ARRIVALS >
ARRIVALS >
HELLO, OFFICER. I AM THR-446.
WELCOME TO THE MOON. MY CAR'S OUTSIDE.

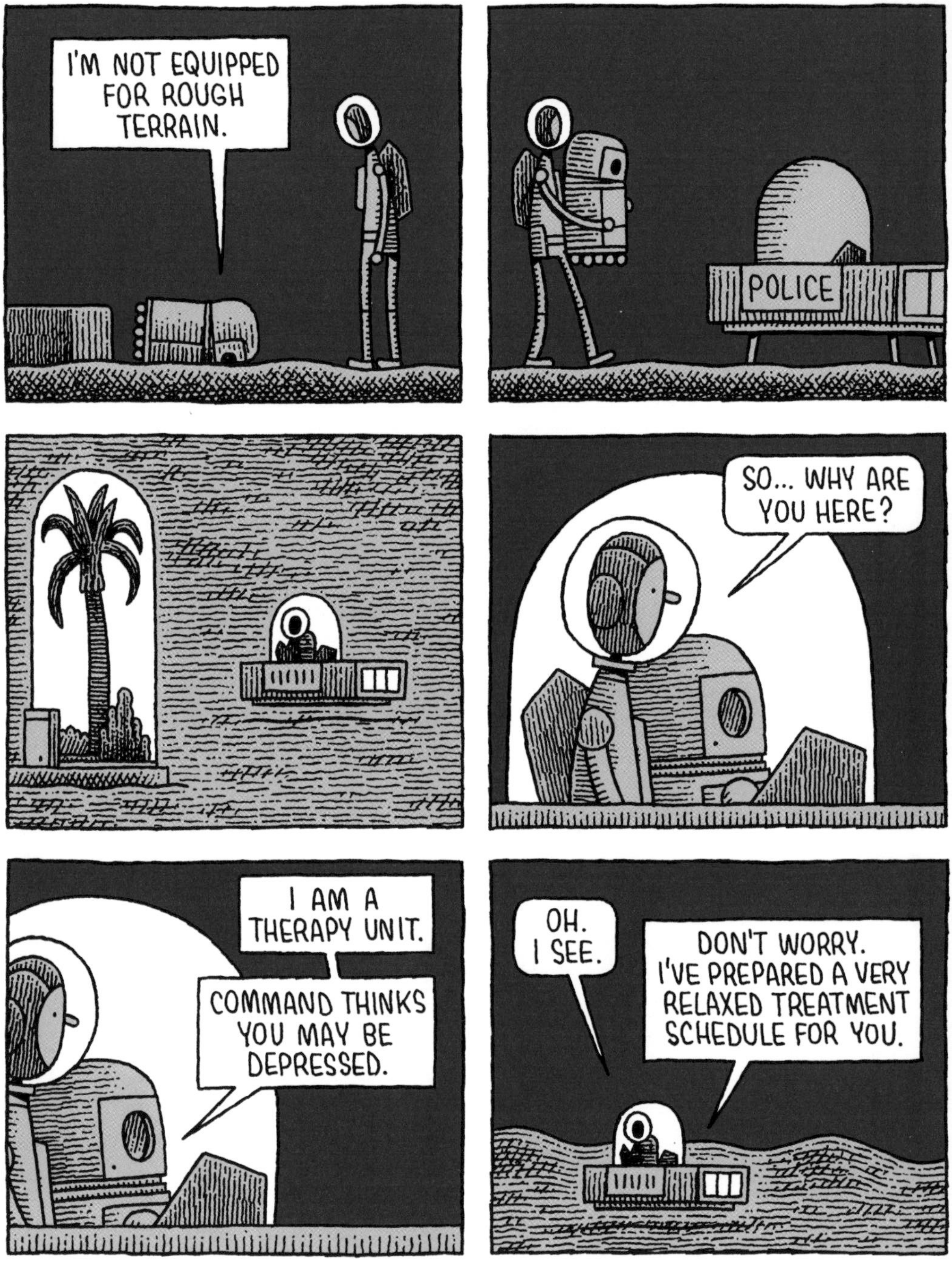
I'M NOT EQUIPPED FOR ROUGH TERRAIN.
POLICE
SO... WHY ARE YOU HERE?
I AM A THERAPY UNIT.
COMMAND THINKS YOU MAY BE DEPRESSED.
OH. I SEE.
DON'T WORRY. I'VE PREPARED A VERY RELAXED TREATMENT SCHEDULE FOR YOU.

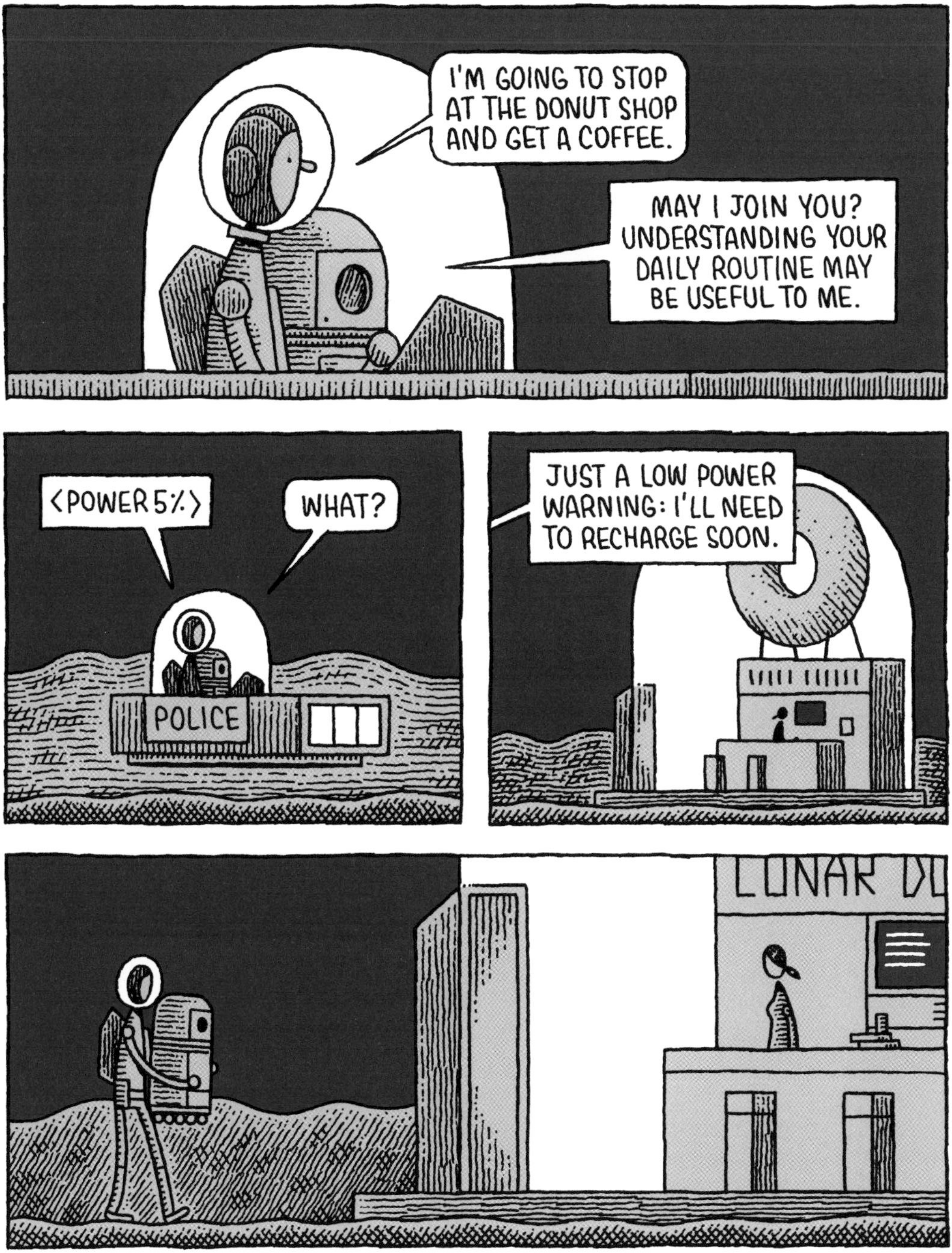
I'M GOING TO STOP AT THE DONUT SHOP AND GET A COFFEE.
MAY I JOIN YOU? UNDERSTANDING YOUR DAILY ROUTINE MAY BE USEFUL TO ME.
<POWER 5%>
WHAT?
POLICE
JUST A LOW POWER WARNING: I'LL NEED TO RECHARGE SOON.
LUNAR D

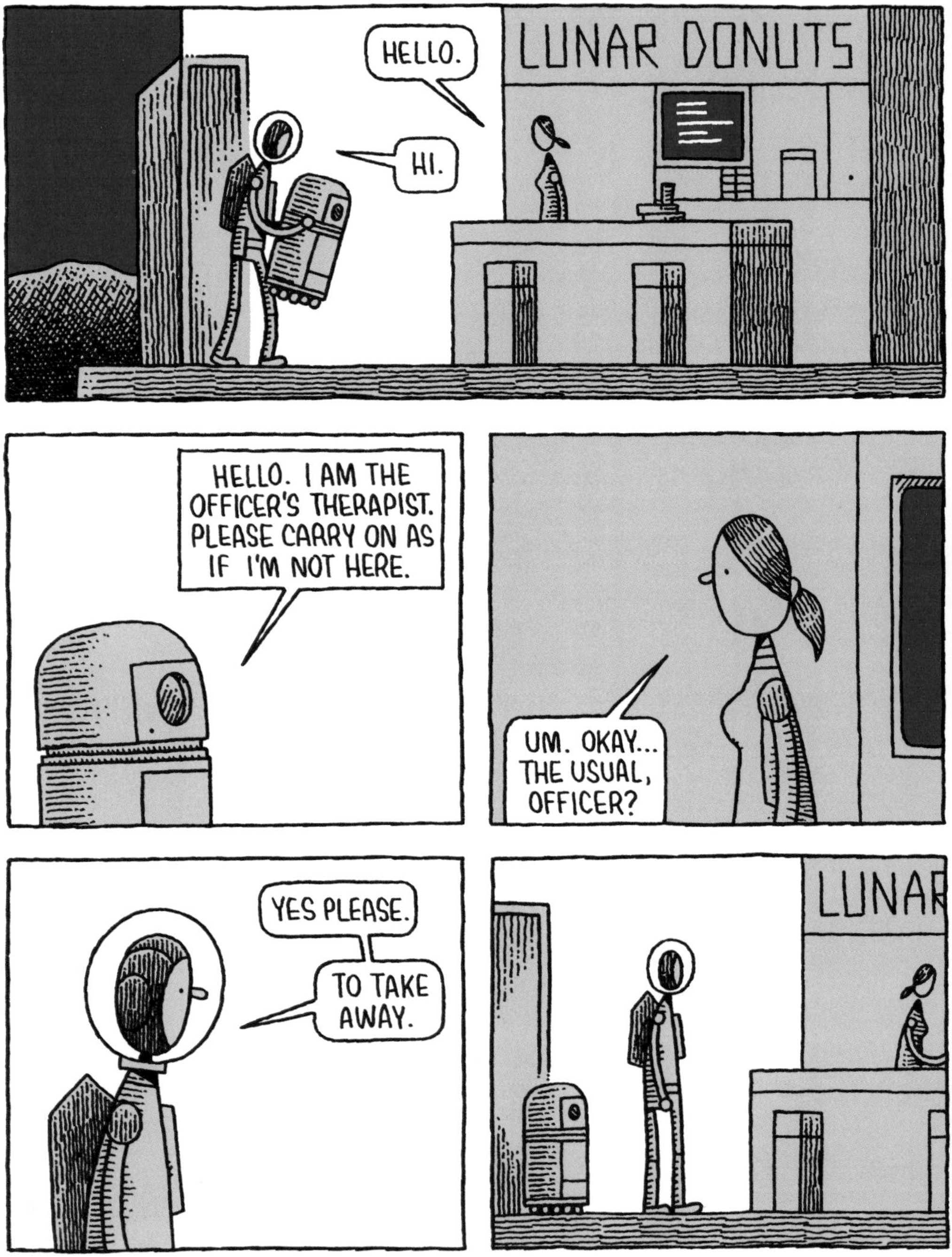

LUNAR DONUTS
HELLO.
HI.
HELLO. I AM THE OFFICER'S THERAPIST. PLEASE CARRY ON AS IF I'M NOT HERE.
UM. OKAY... THE USUAL, OFFICER?
YES PLEASE.
TO TAKE AWAY.
LUNAR

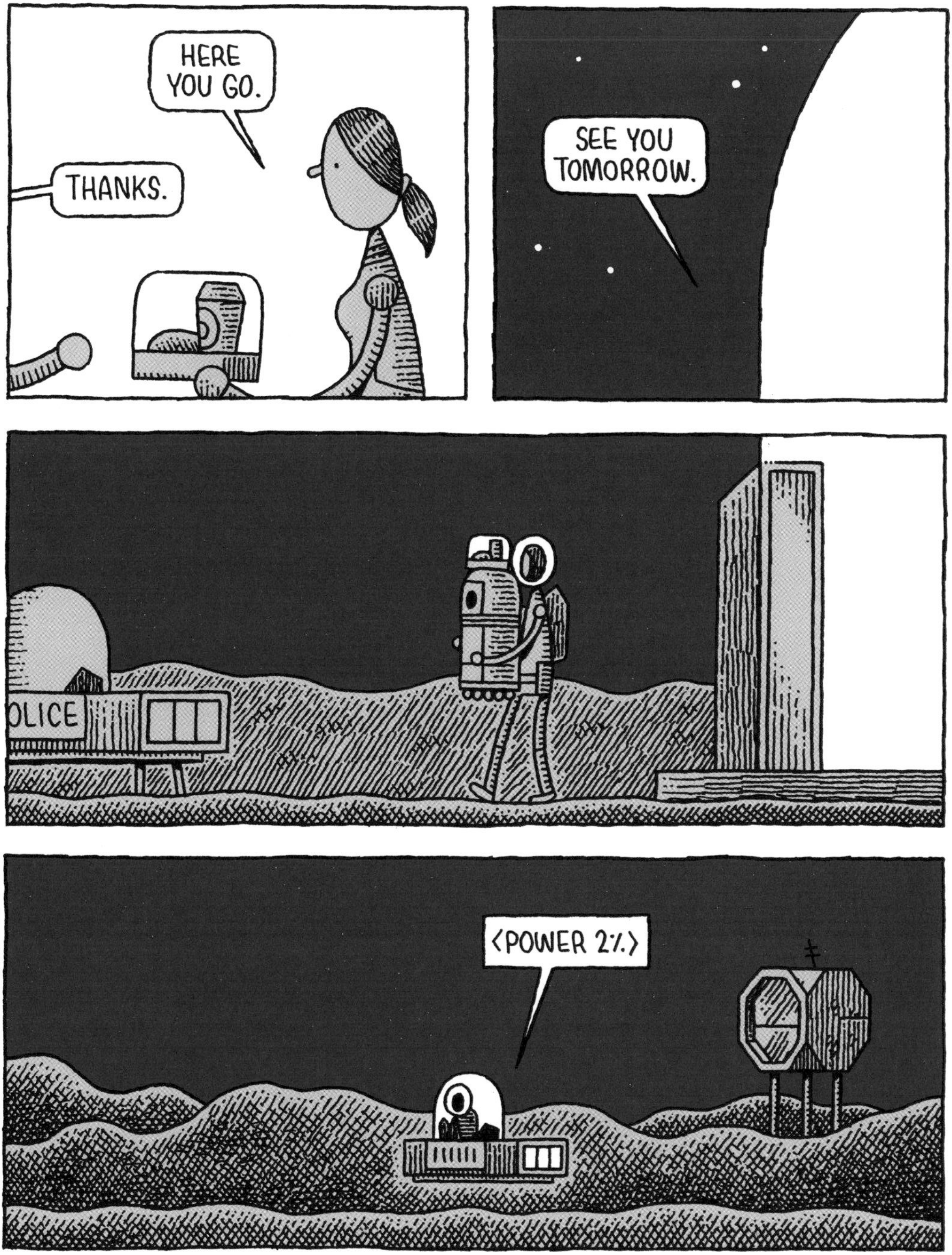
HERE YOU GO.
THANKS.
SEE YOU TOMORROW.
OLICE
<POWER 2%.>

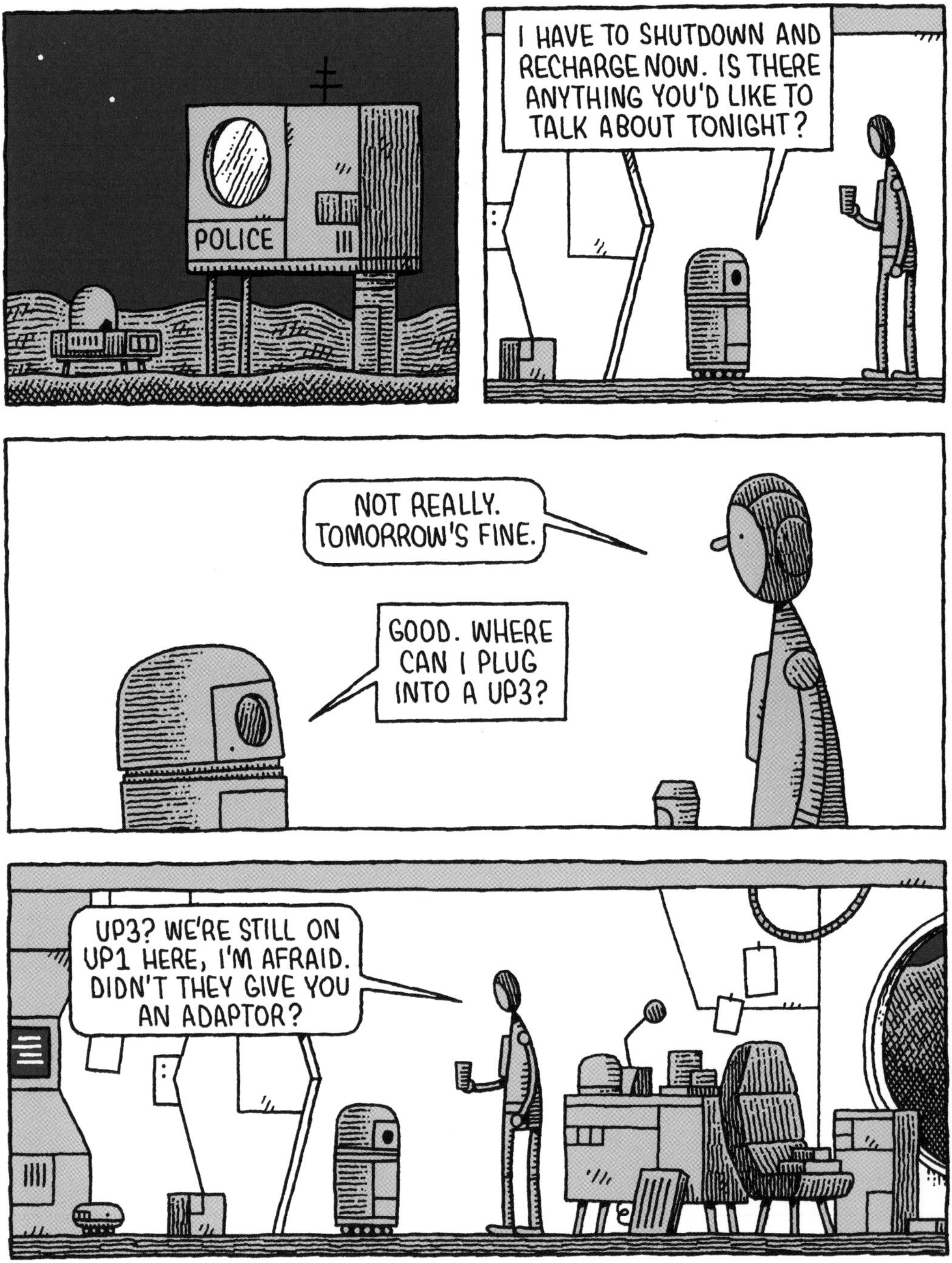
POLICE
I HAVE TO SHUTDOWN AND RECHARGE NOW. IS THERE ANYTHING YOU'D LIKE TO TALK ABOUT TONIGHT?
NOT REALLY. TOMORROW'S FINE.
GOOD. WHERE CAN I PLUG INTO A UP3?
UP3? WE'RE STILL ON UP1 HERE, I'M AFRAID. DIDN'T THEY GIVE YOU AN ADAPTOR?

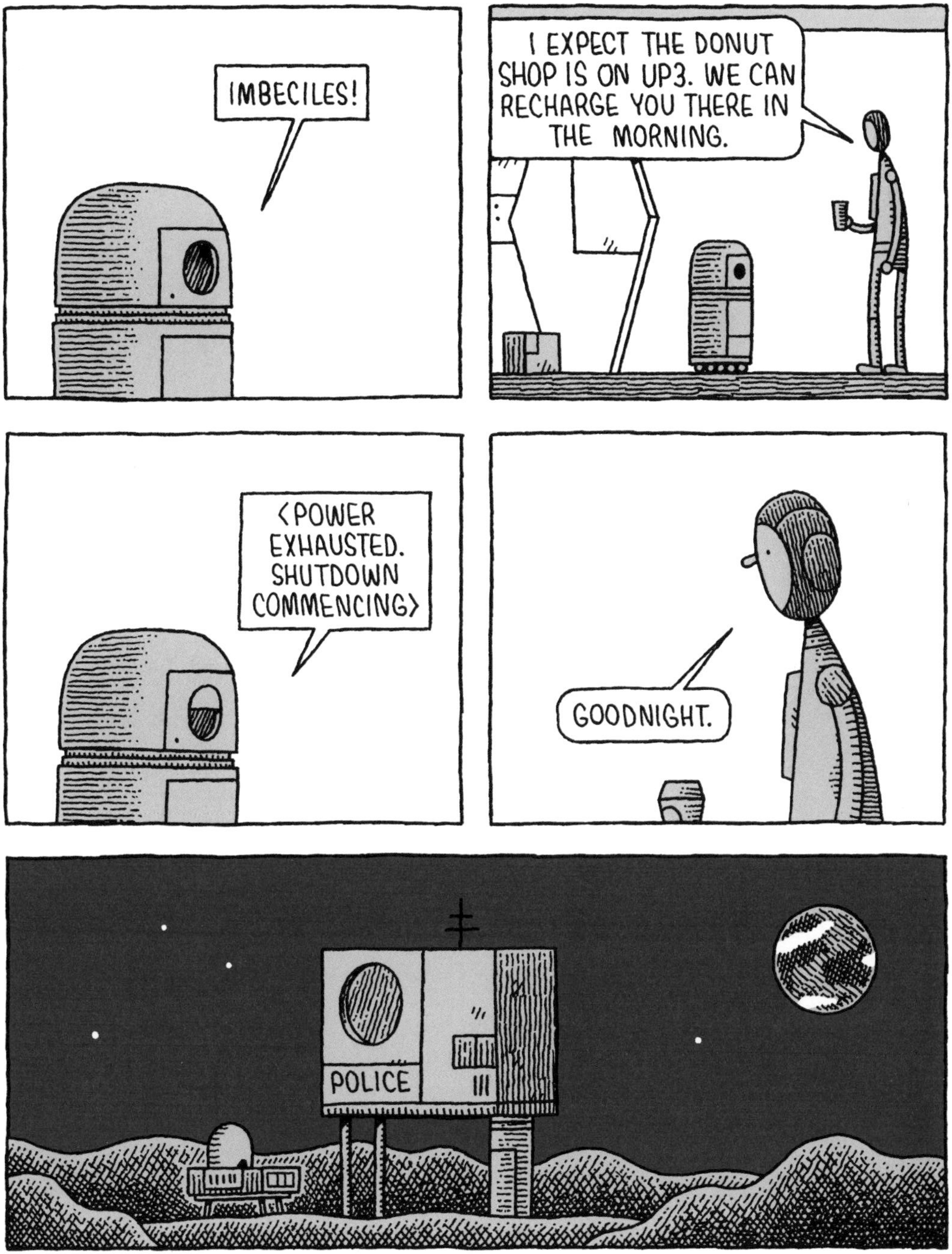
IMBECILES!
I EXPECT THE DONUT SHOP IS ON UP3. WE CAN RECHARGE YOU THERE IN THE MORNING.
<POWER EXHAUSTED. SHUTDOWN COMMENCING>
GOODNIGHT.
POLICE

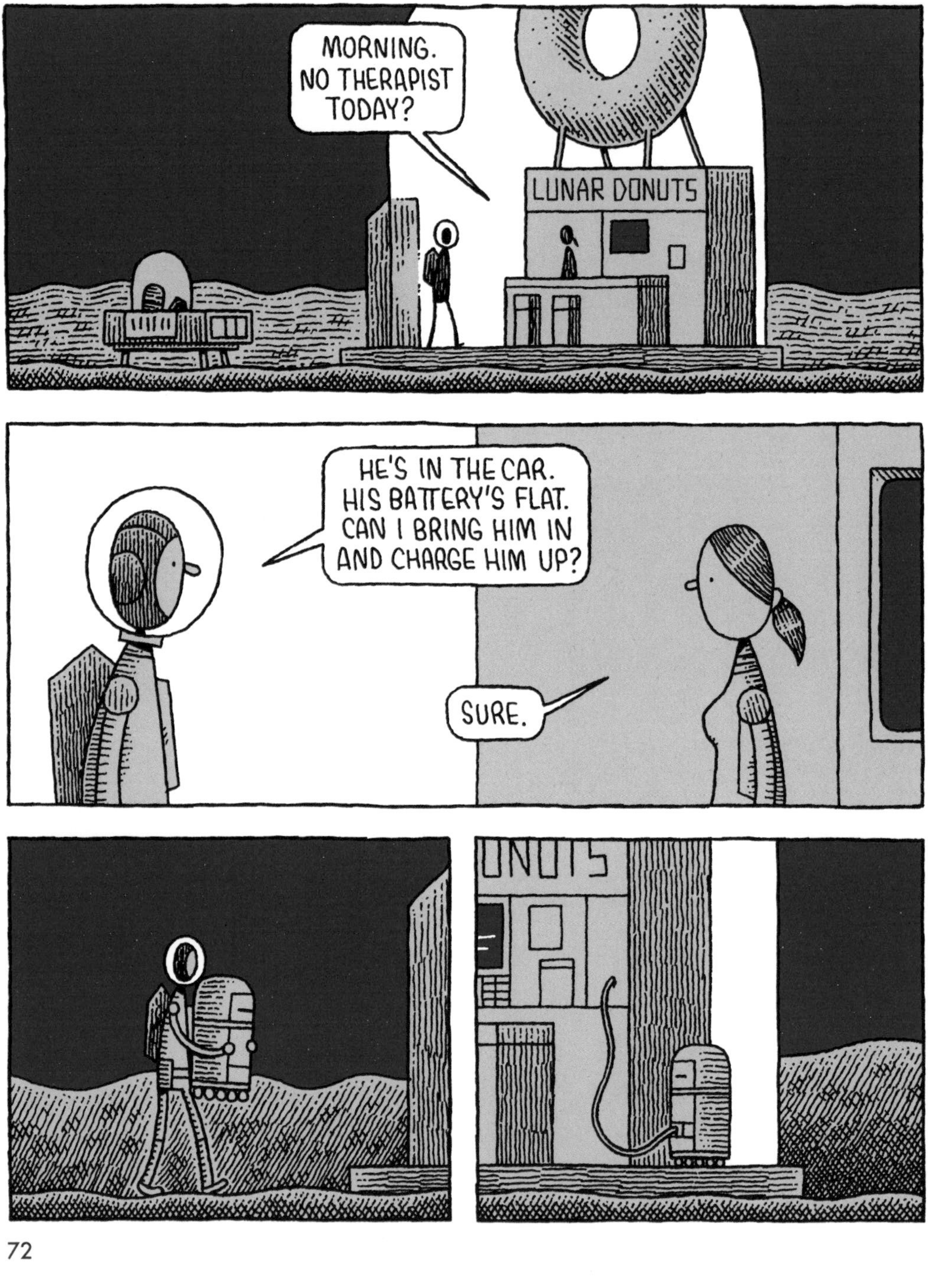
MORNING. NO THERAPIST TODAY?
LUNAR DONUTS
HE'S IN THE CAR. HIS BATTERY'S FLAT. CAN I BRING HIM IN AND CHARGE HIM UP?
SURE.
ONUTS

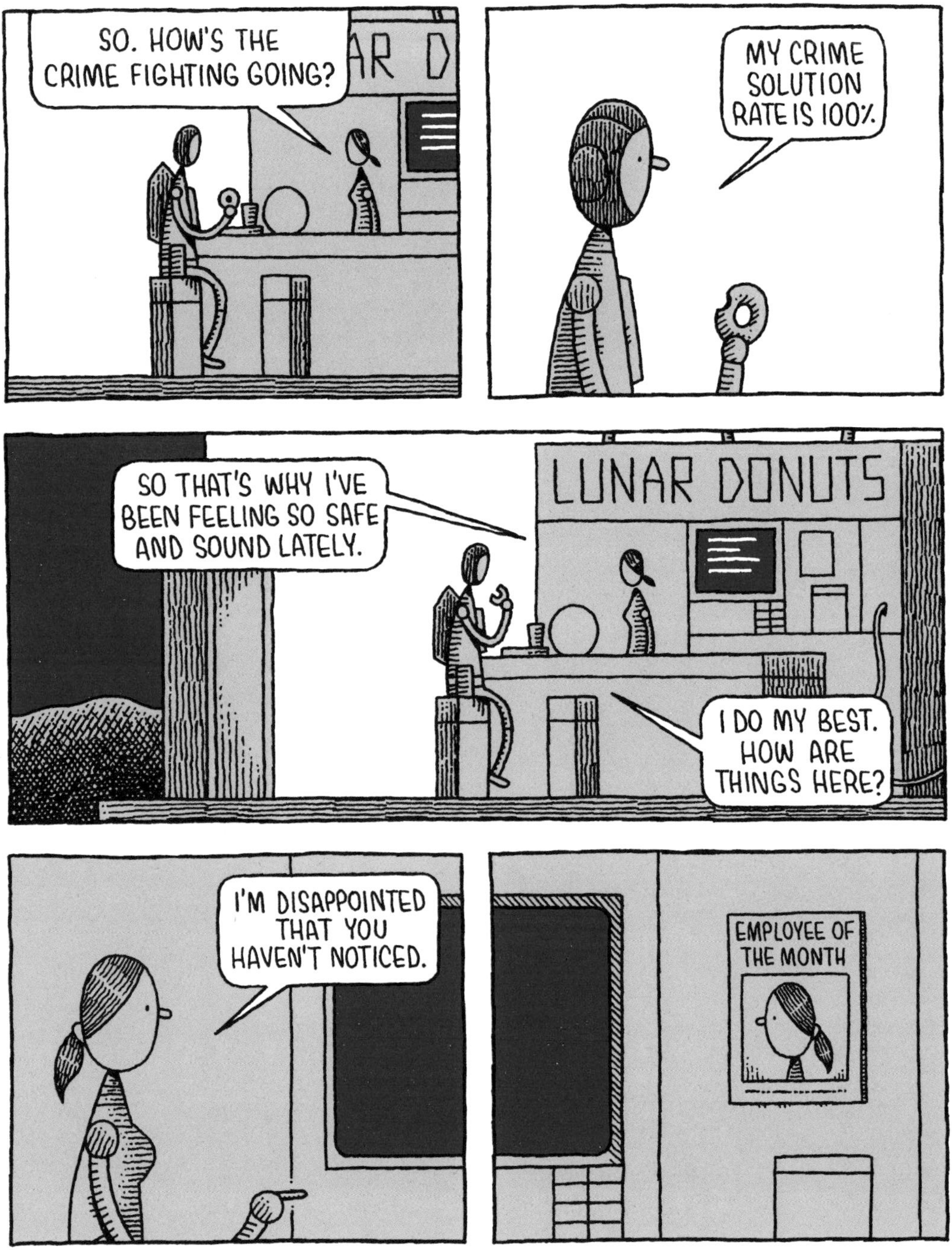
SO. HOW'S THE CRIME FIGHTING GOING?
AR D
MY CRIME SOLUTION RATE IS 100%.
SO THAT'S WHY I'VE BEEN FEELING SO SAFE AND SOUND LATELY.
LUNAR DONUTS
I DO MY BEST. HOW ARE THINGS HERE?
I'M DISAPPOINTED THAT YOU HAVEN'T NOTICED.
EMPLOYEE OF THE MONTH

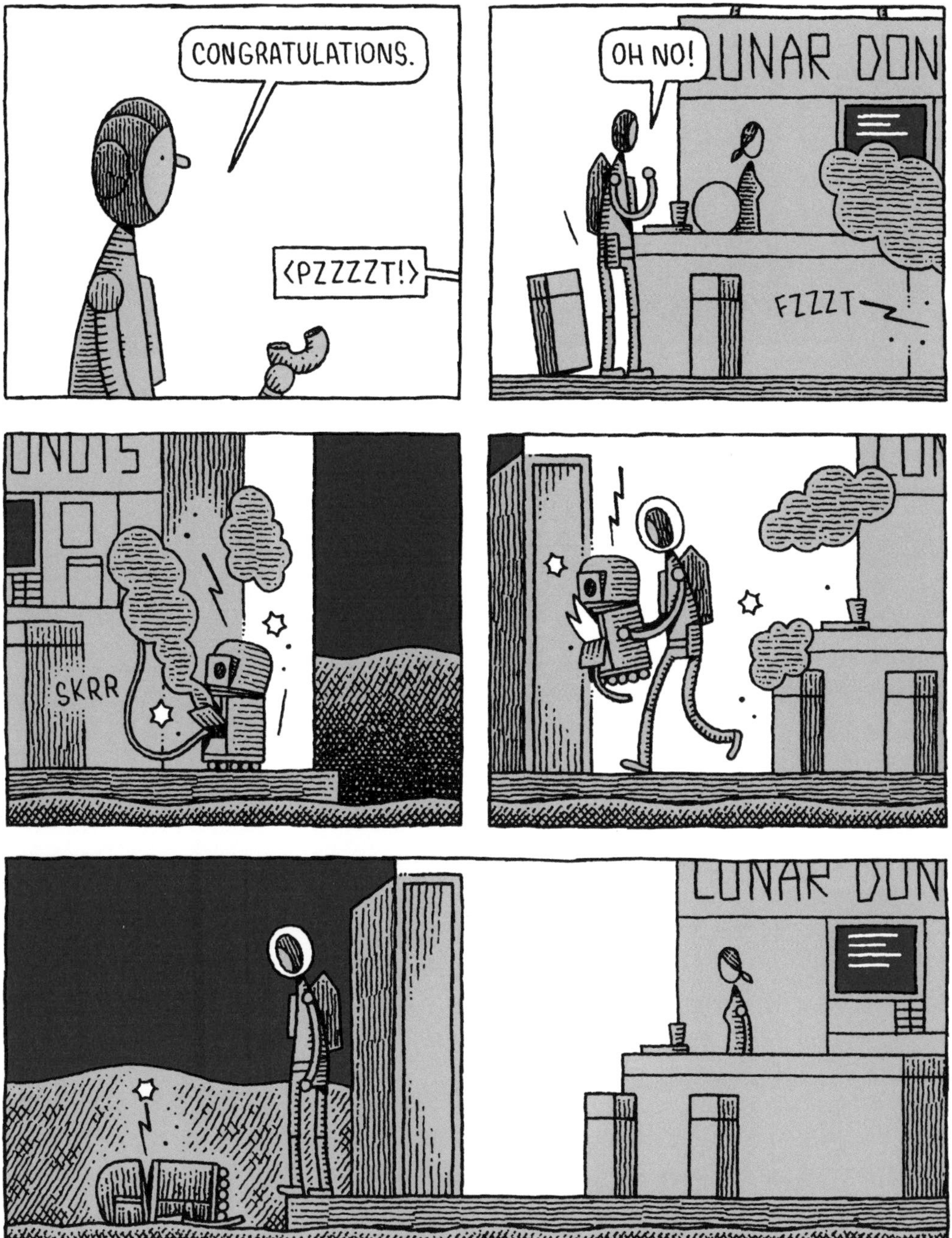
CONGRATULATIONS.
<PZZZZT!>
OH NO!
LUNAR DON
FZZZT
SKRR
LUNAR DON

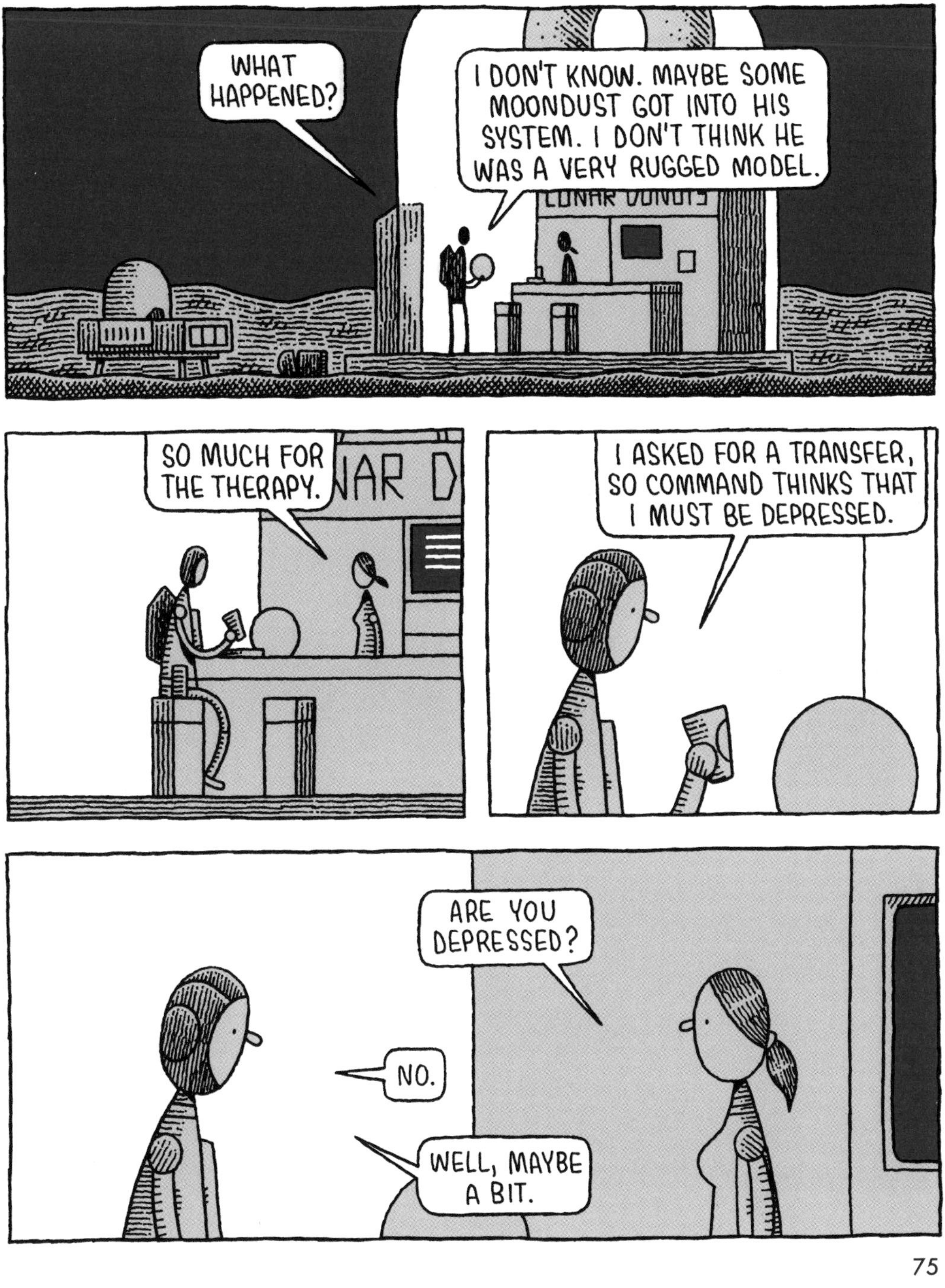
WHAT HAPPENED?
I DON'T KNOW. MAYBE SOME MOONDUST GOT INTO HIS SYSTEM. I DON'T THINK HE WAS A VERY RUGGED MODEL.
LUNAR DONUTS
SO MUCH FOR THE THERAPY.
I ASKED FOR A TRANSFER, SO COMMAND THINKS THAT I MUST BE DEPRESSED.
ARE YOU DEPRESSED?
NO.
WELL, MAYBE A BIT.

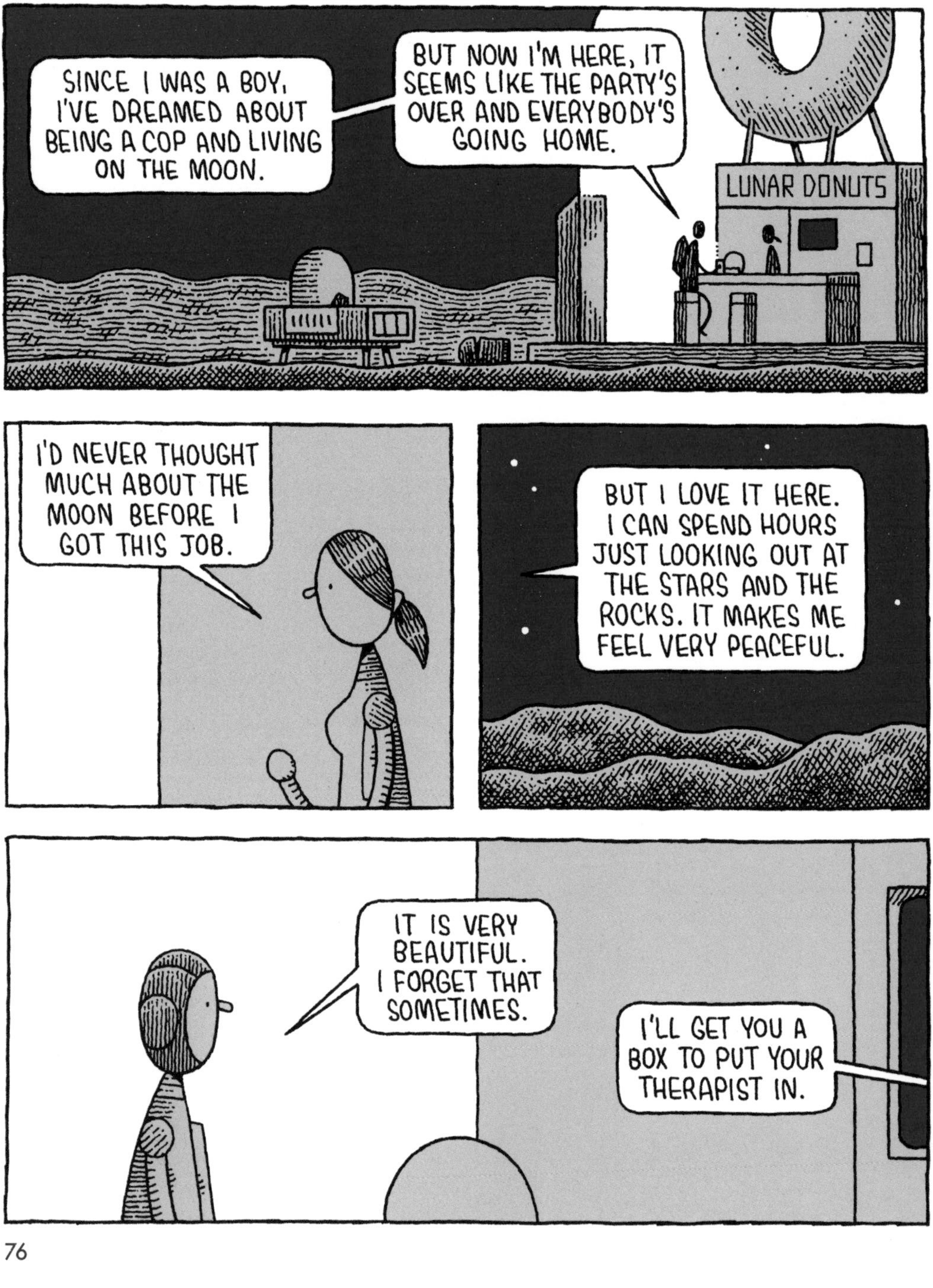
SINCE I WAS A BOY, I'VE DREAMED ABOUT BEING A COP AND LIVING ON THE MOON.
BUT NOW I'M HERE, IT SEEMS LIKE THE PARTY'S OVER AND EVERYBODY'S GOING HOME.
LUNAR DONUTS
I'D NEVER THOUGHT MUCH ABOUT THE MOON BEFORE I GOT THIS JOB.
BUT I LOVE IT HERE. I CAN SPEND HOURS JUST LOOKING OUT AT THE STARS AND THE ROCKS. IT MAKES ME FEEL VERY PEACEFUL.
IT IS VERY BEAUTIFUL. I FORGET THAT SOMETIMES.
I'LL GET YOU A BOX TO PUT YOUR THERAPIST IN.

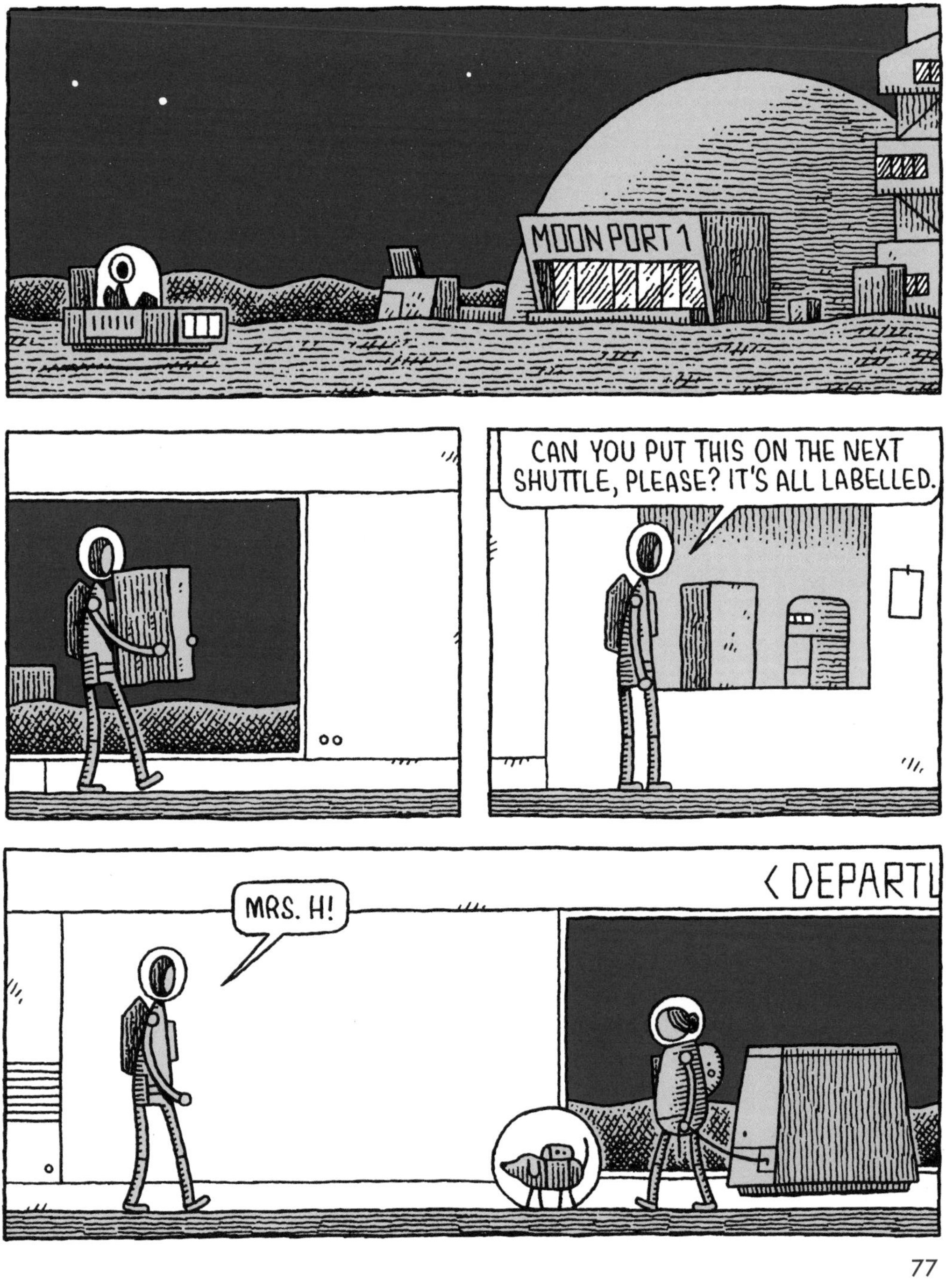
MOON PORT 1
CAN YOU PUT THIS ON THE NEXT SHUTTLE, PLEASE? IT'S ALL LABELLED.
< DEPARTU
MRS. H!

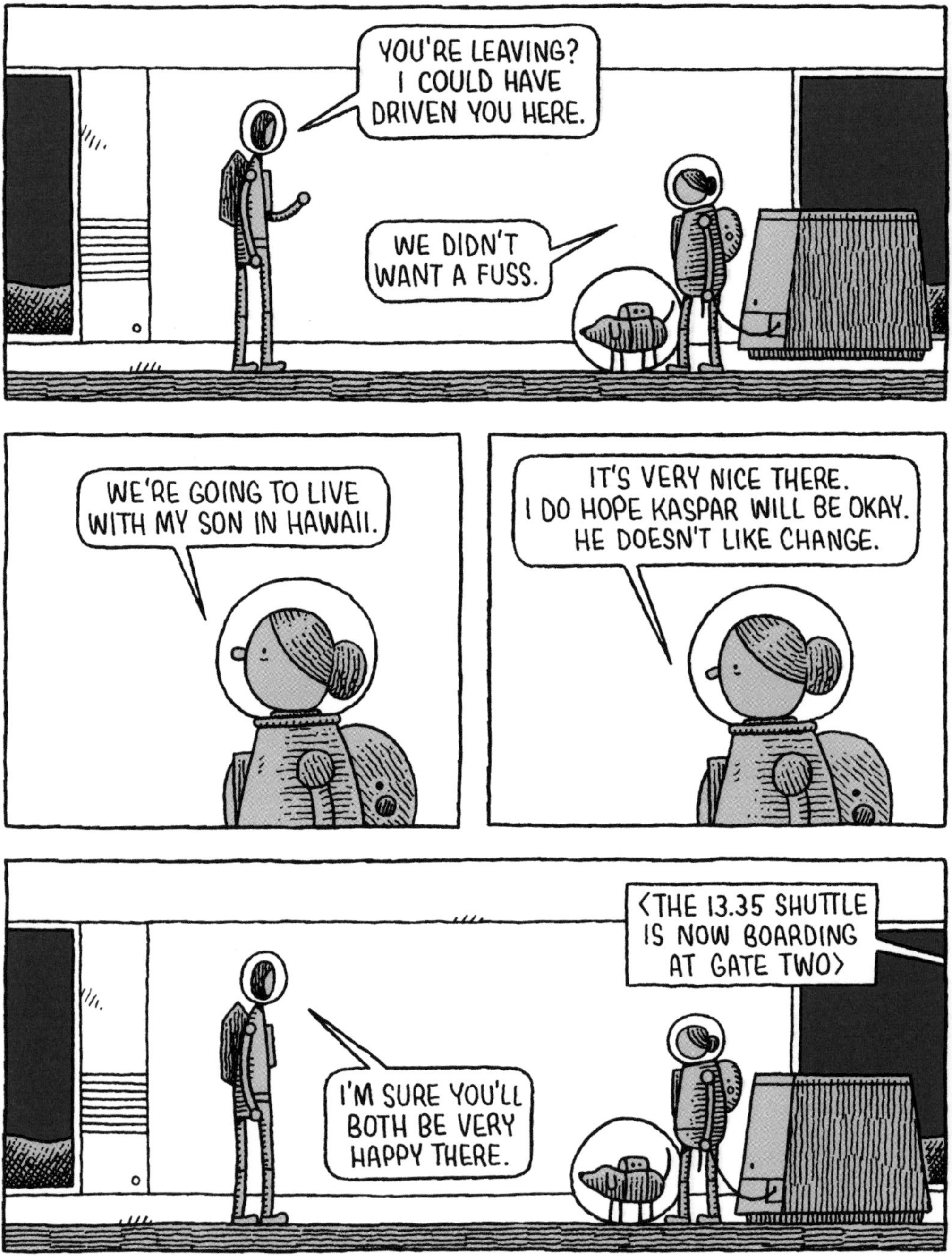
YOU'RE LEAVING? I COULD HAVE DRIVEN YOU HERE.
WE DIDN'T WANT A FUSS.
WE'RE GOING TO LIVE WITH MY SON IN HAWAII.
IT'S VERY NICE THERE. I DO HOPE KASPAR WILL BE OKAY. HE DOESN'T LIKE CHANGE.
<THE 13.35 SHUTTLE IS NOW BOARDING AT GATE TWO>
I'M SURE YOU'LL BOTH BE VERY HAPPY THERE.

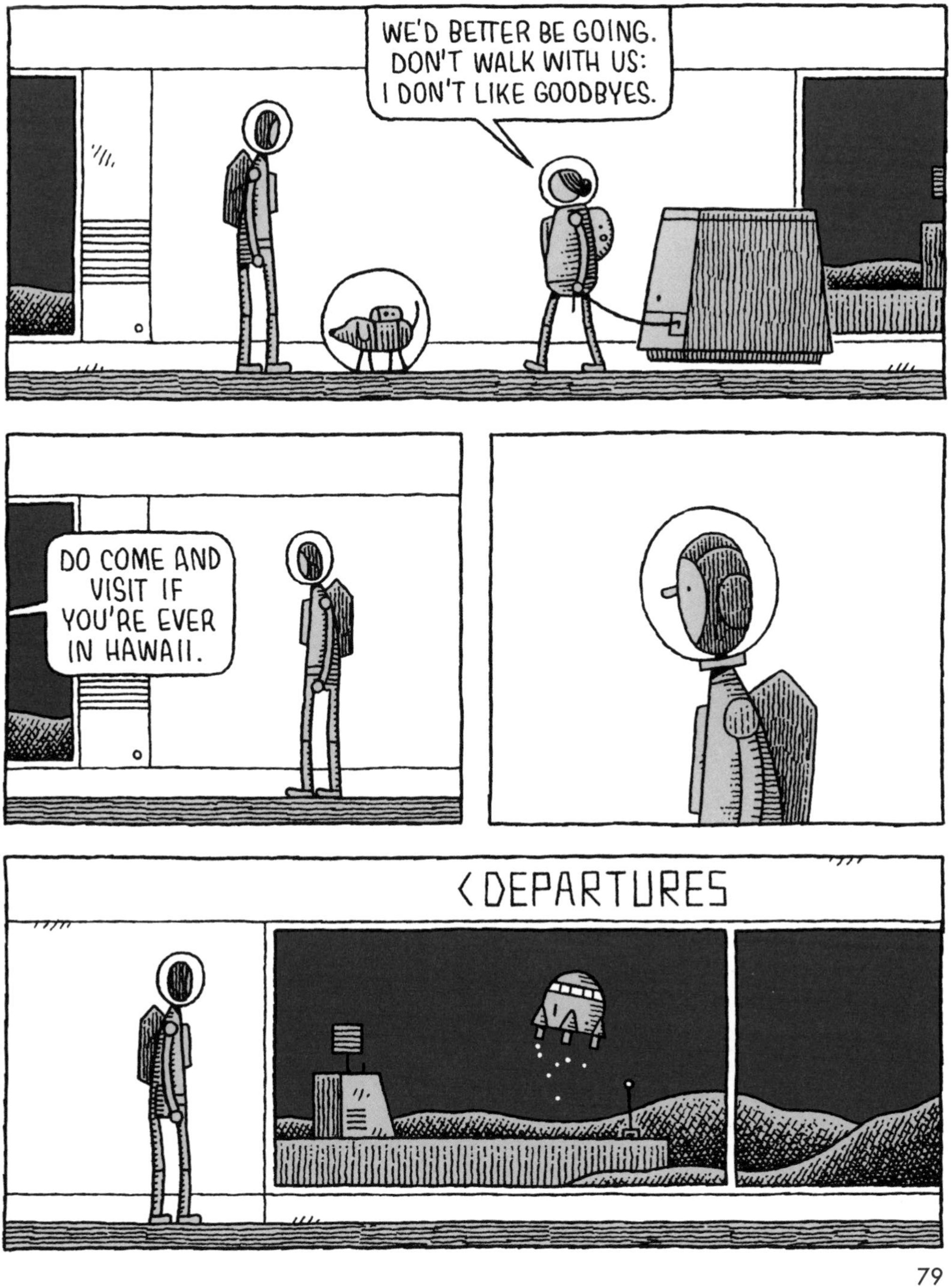
WE'D BETTER BE GOING. DON'T WALK WITH US: I DON'T LIKE GOODBYES.
DO COME AND VISIT IF YOU'RE EVER IN HAWAII.
⟨DEPARTURES

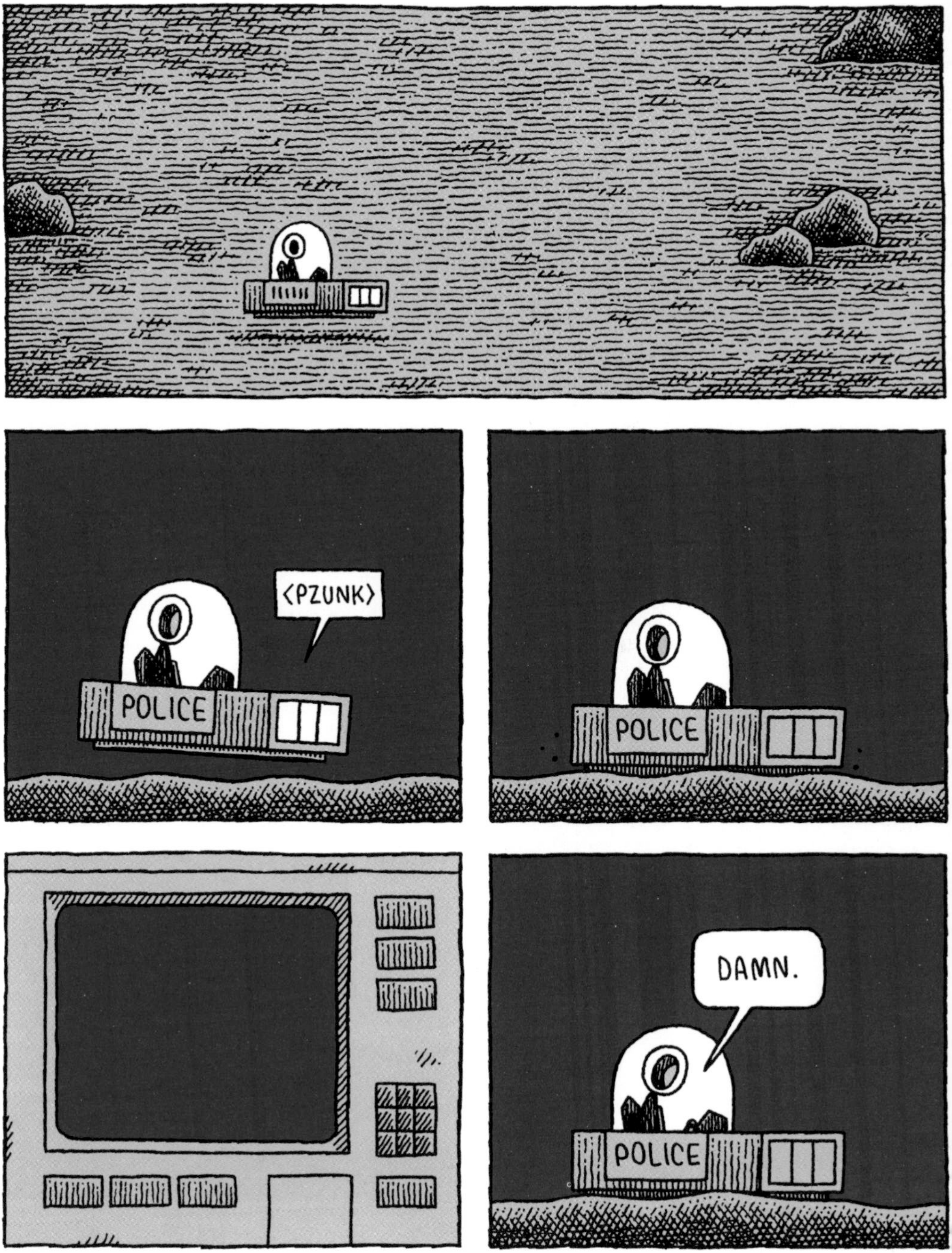
<PZUNK>
POLICE
POLICE
POLICE
DAMN.

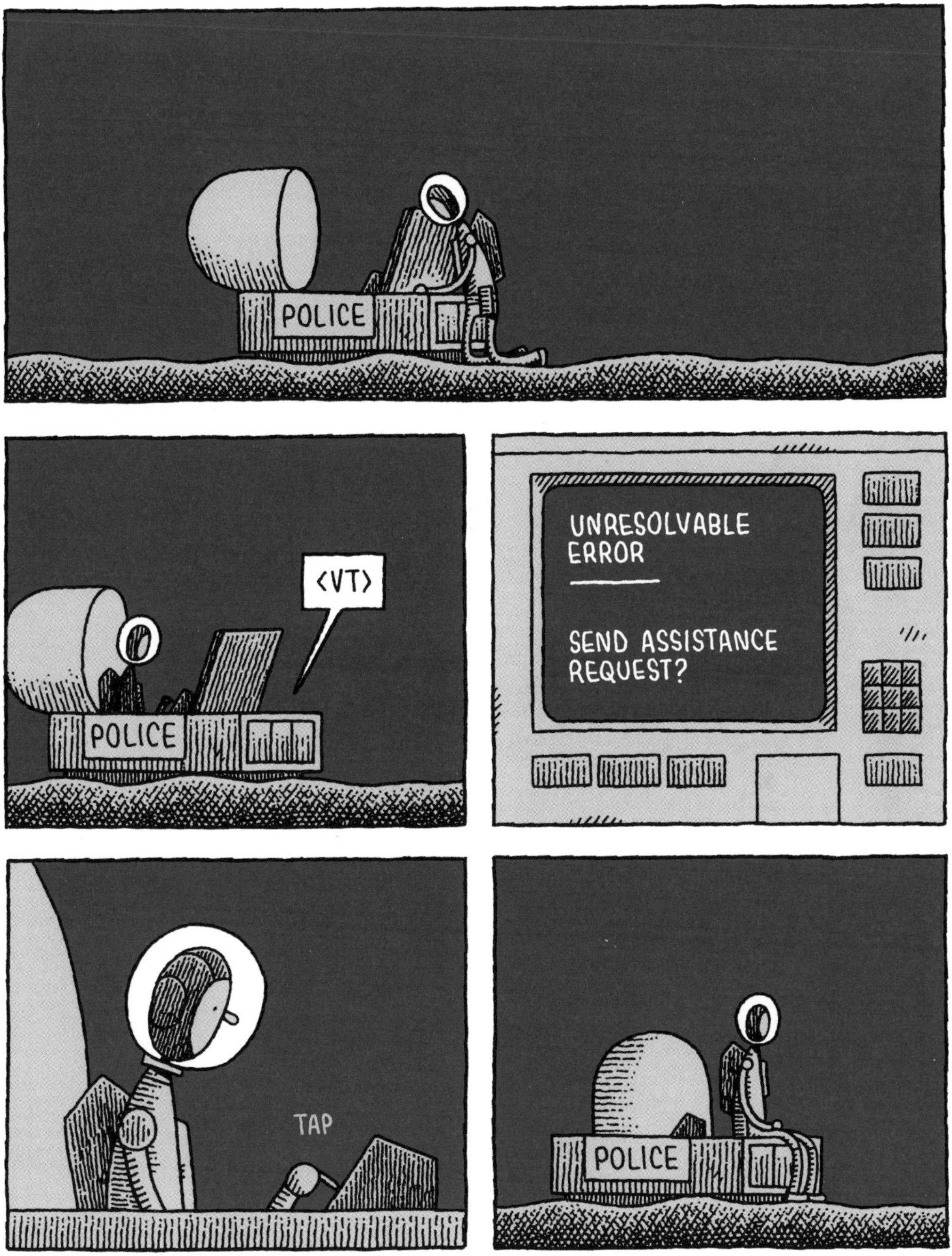
POLICE
<VT>
POLICE
UNRESOLVABLE ERROR
SEND ASSISTANCE REQUEST?
TAP
POLICE

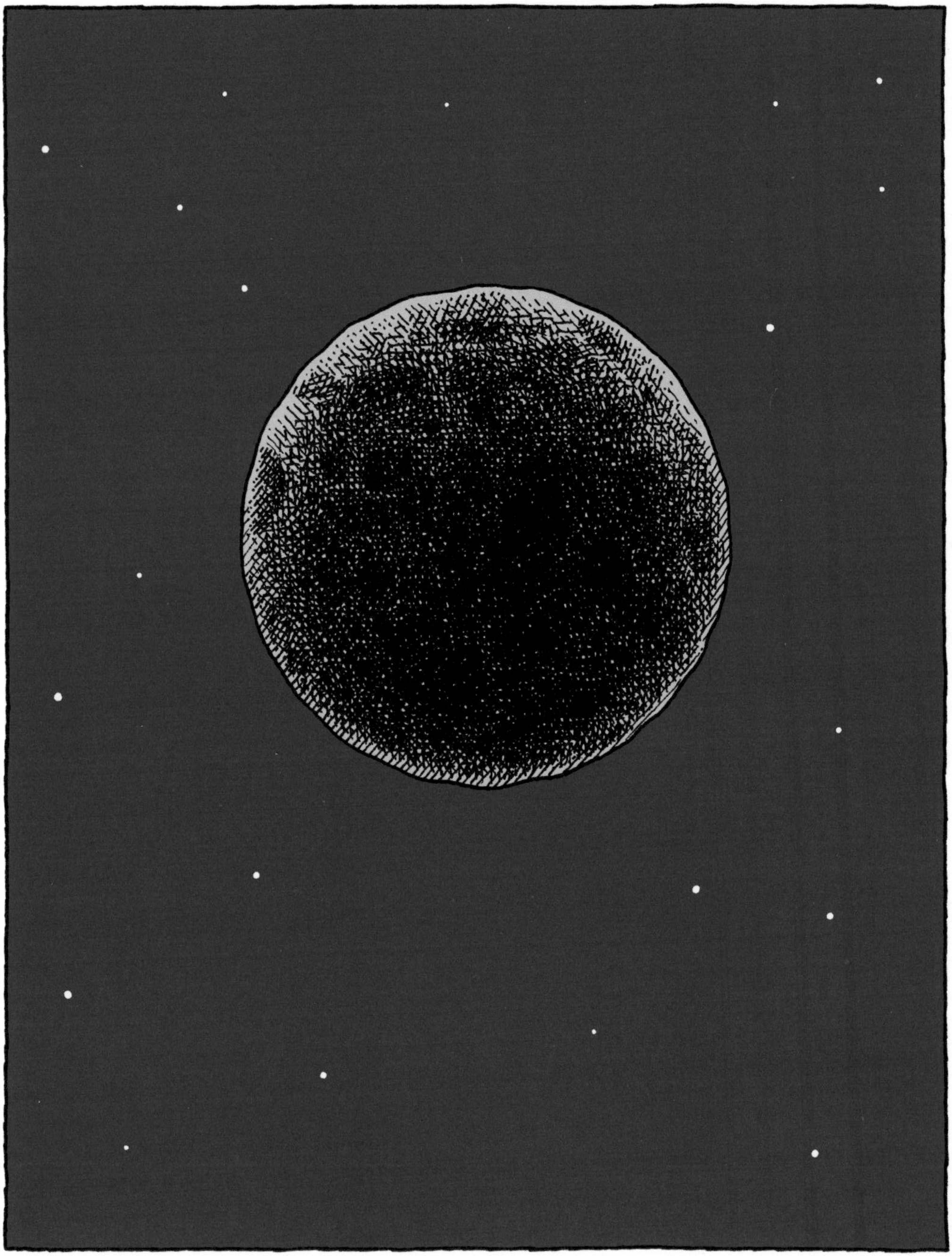

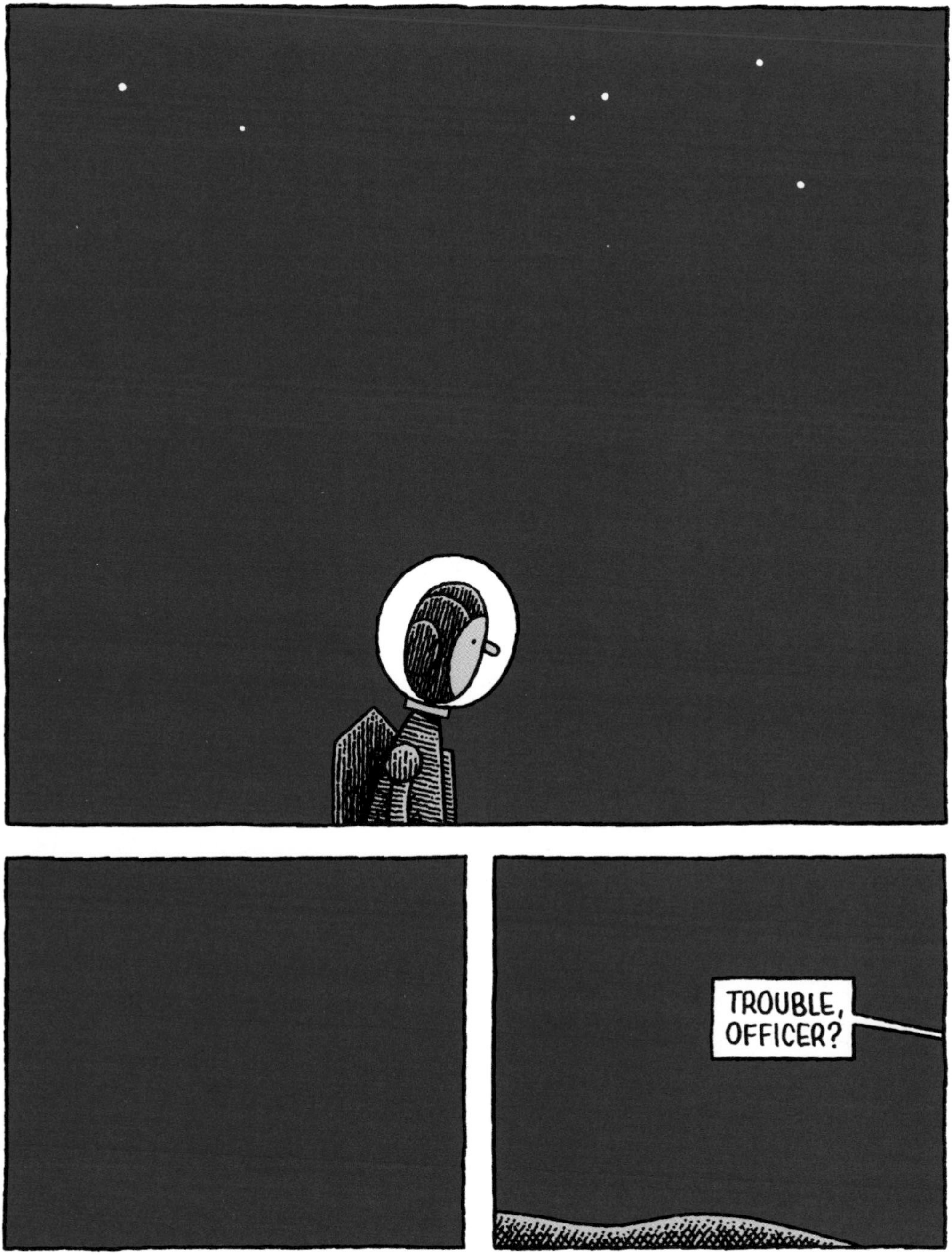
TROUBLE,
OFFICER?

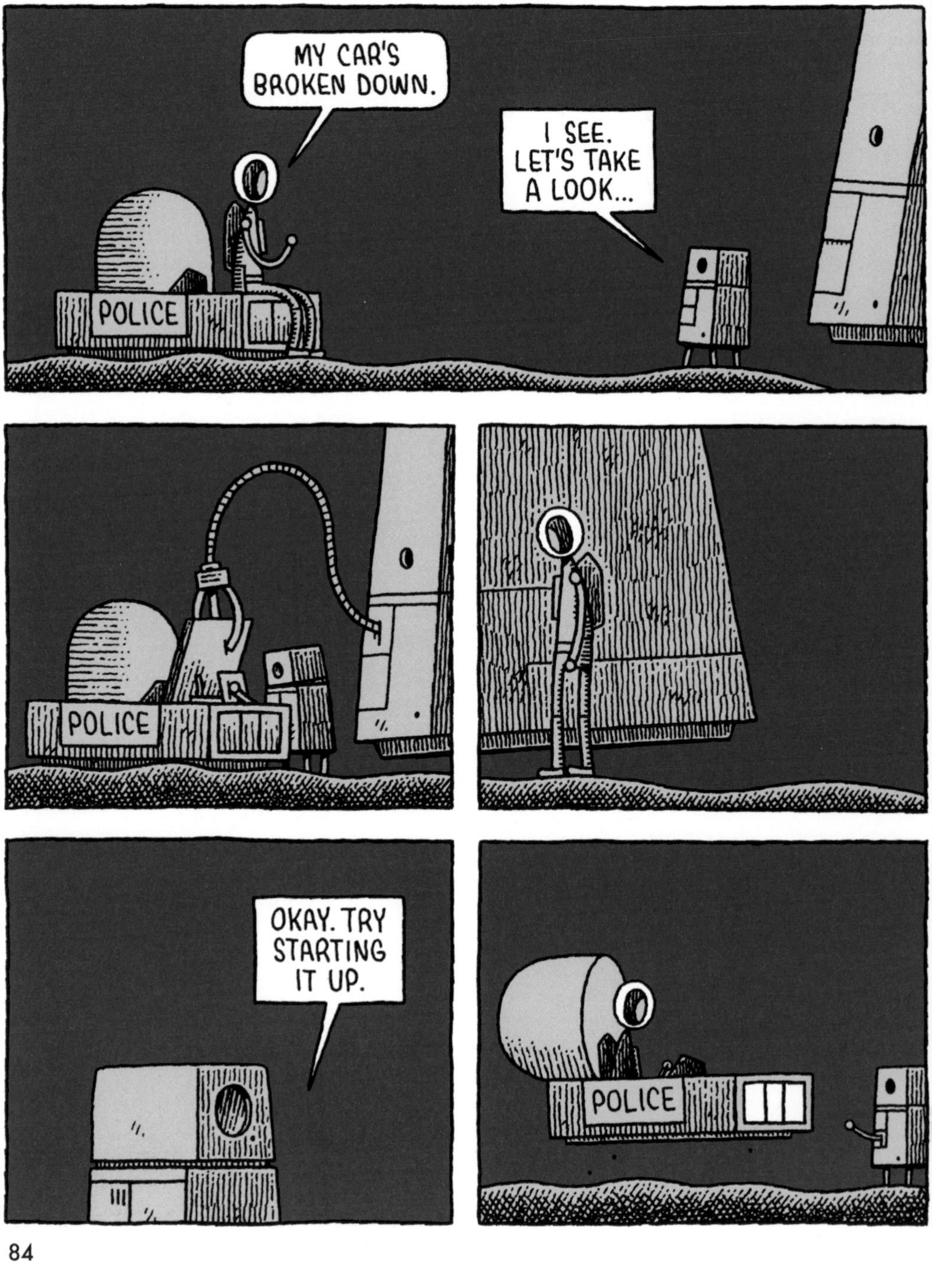
MY CAR'S BROKEN DOWN.
I SEE. LET'S TAKE A LOOK...
POLICE
POLICE
OKAY. TRY STARTING IT UP.
POLICE

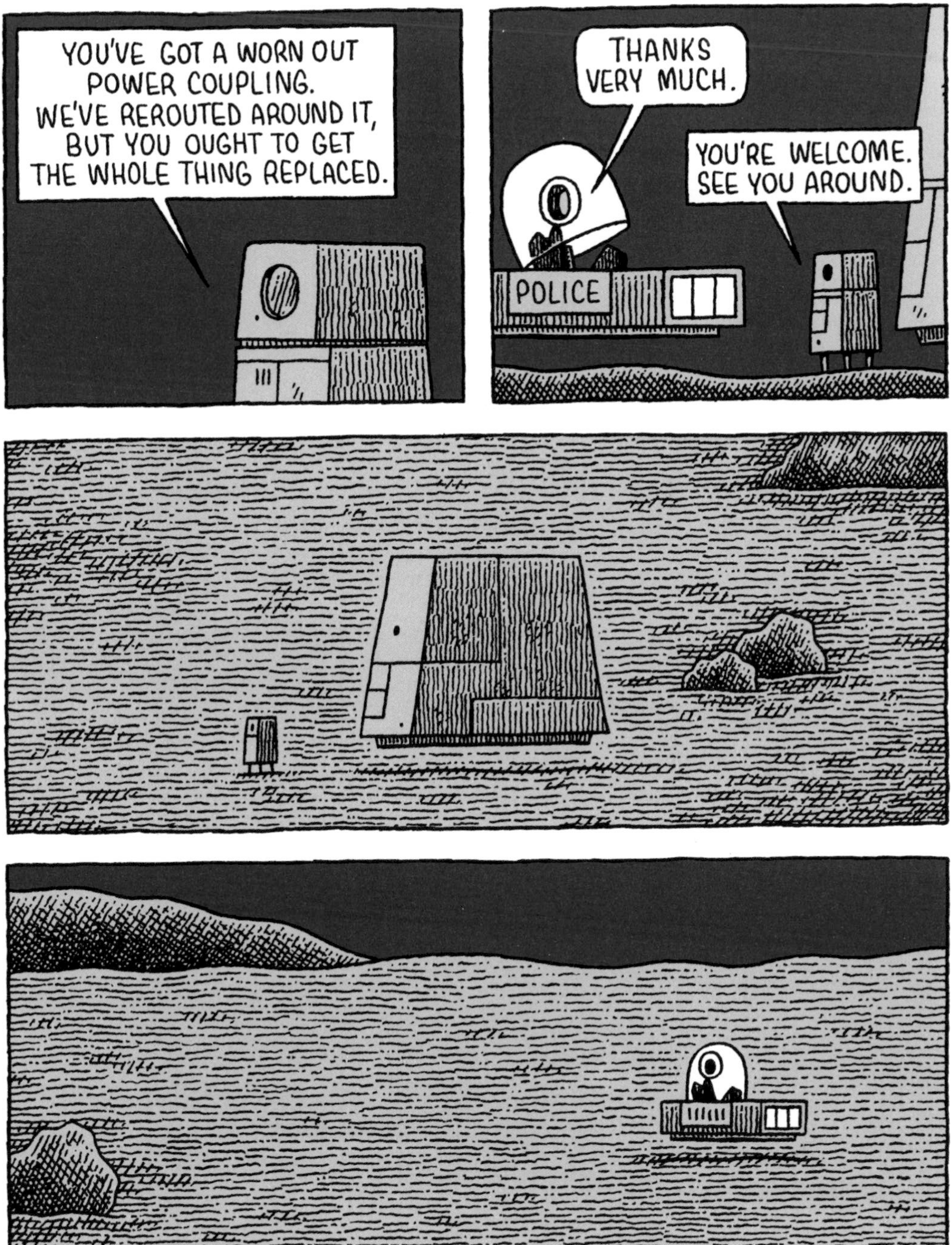
YOU'VE GOT A WORN OUT POWER COUPLING. WE'VE REROUTED AROUND IT, BUT YOU OUGHT TO GET THE WHOLE THING REPLACED.
THANKS VERY MUCH.
YOU'RE WELCOME. SEE YOU AROUND.
POLICE

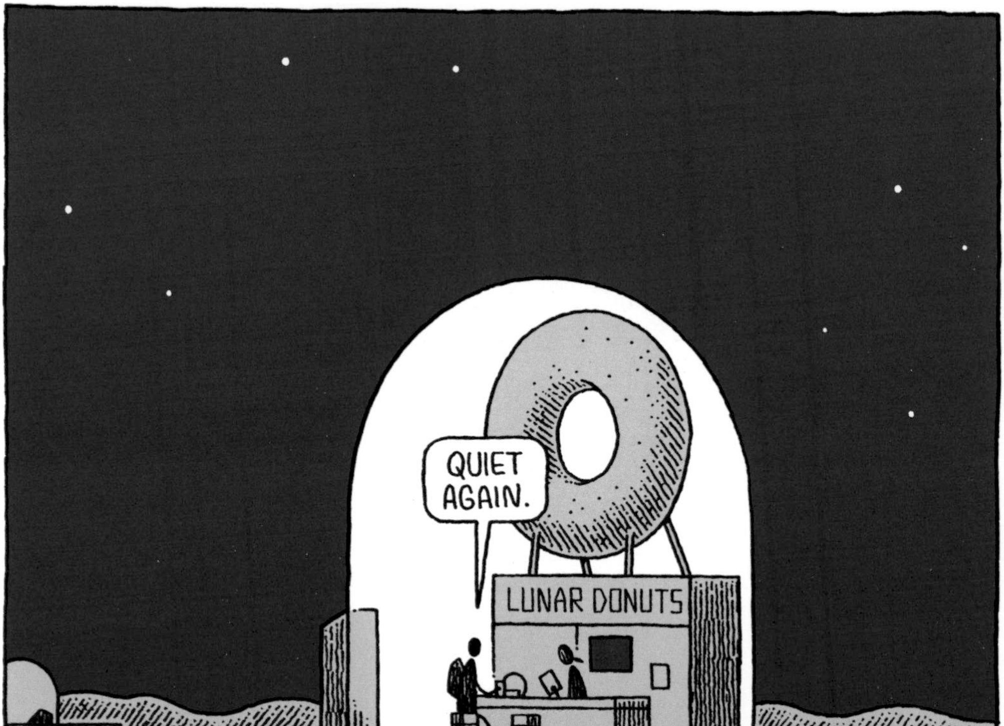
QUIET AGAIN.
LUNAR DONUTS

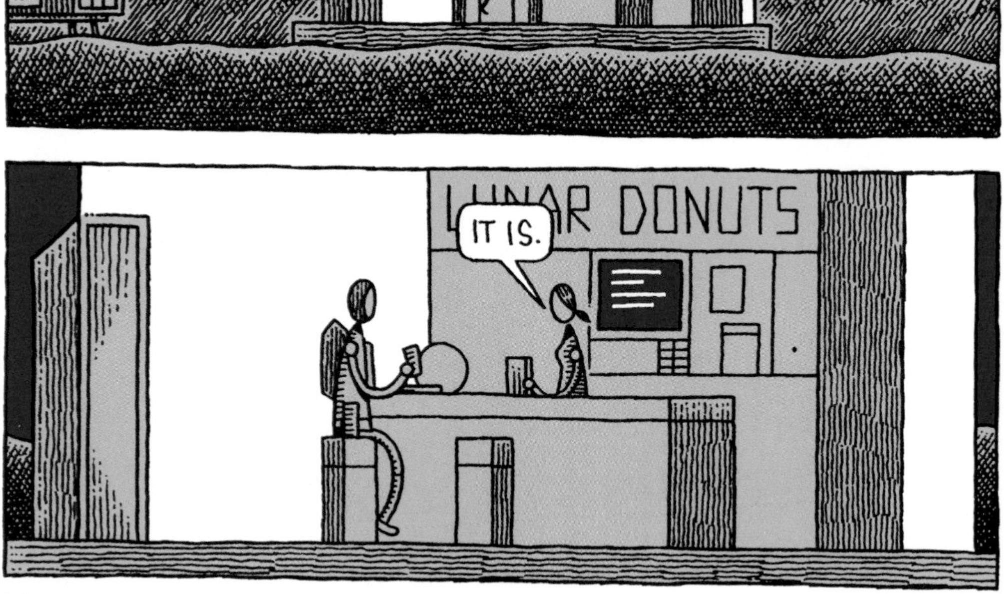
IT IS.

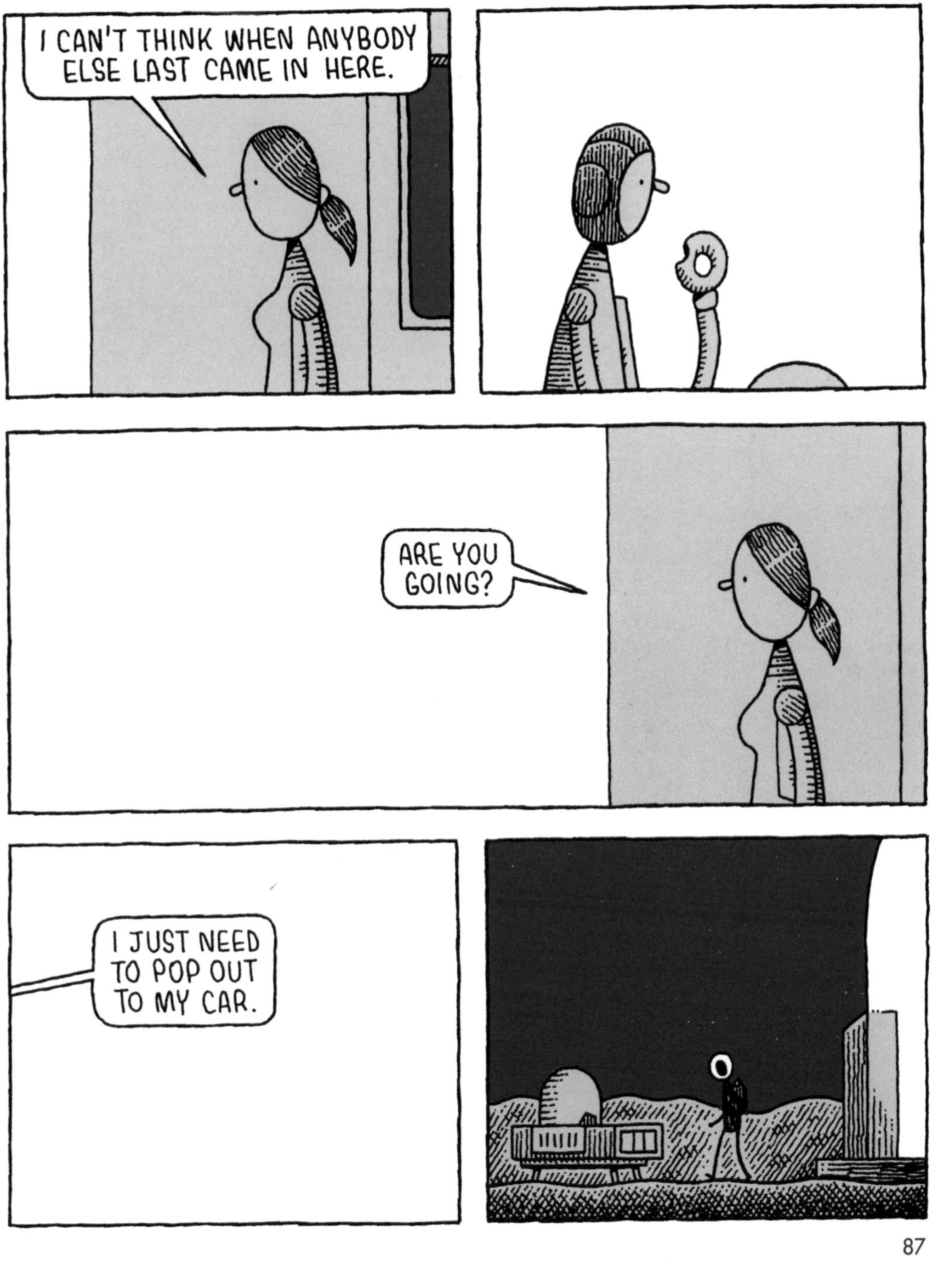
I CAN'T THINK WHEN ANYBODY ELSE LAST CAME IN HERE.
ARE YOU GOING?
I JUST NEED TO POP OUT TO MY CAR.

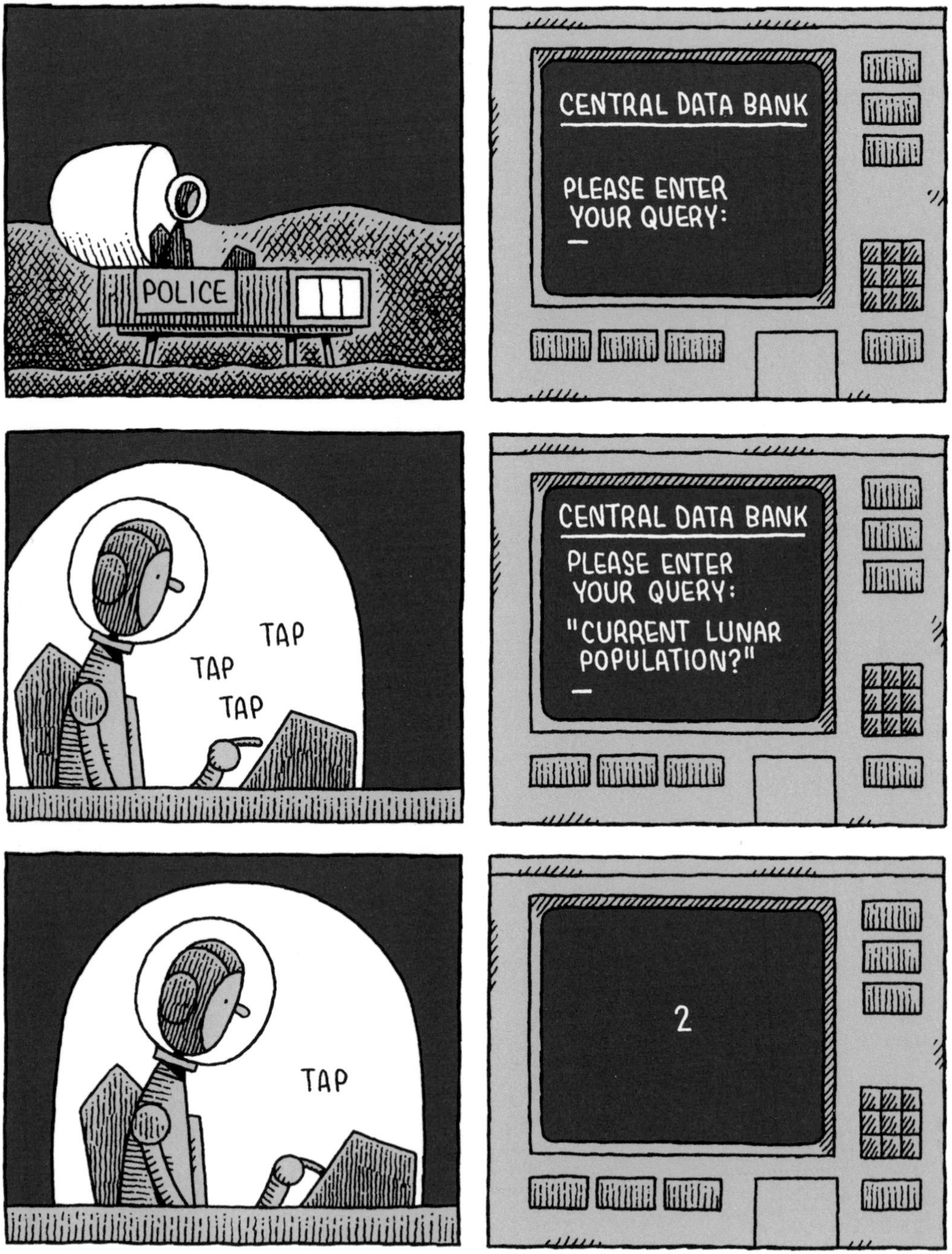
POLICE
CENTRAL DATA BANK
PLEASE ENTER
YOUR QUERY:
TAP
TAP
TAP
CENTRAL DATA BANK
PLEASE ENTER
YOUR QUERY:
"CURRENT LUNAR
POPULATION?"
TAP
2

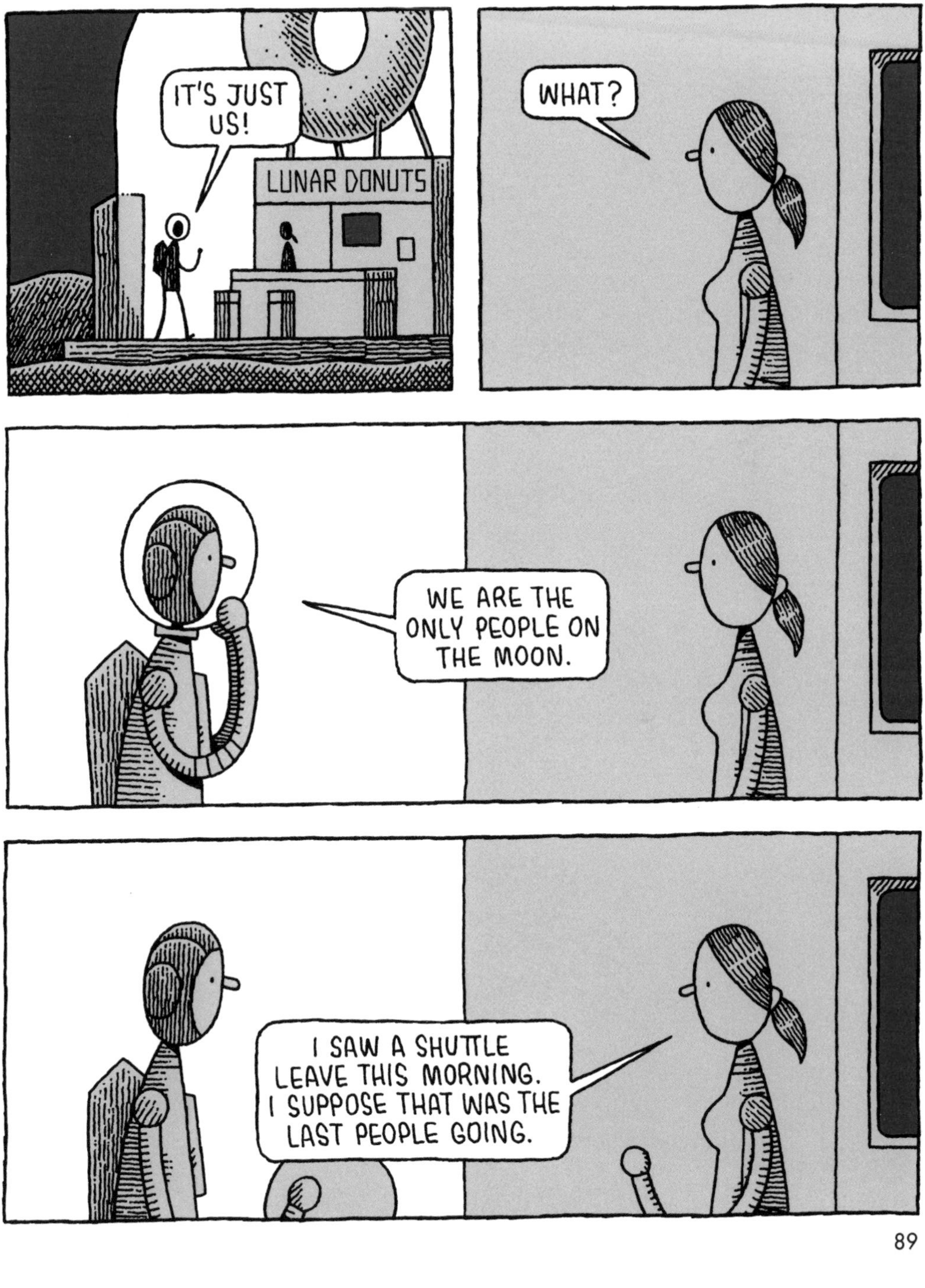
IT'S JUST US!
LUNAR DONUTS
WHAT?
WE ARE THE ONLY PEOPLE ON THE MOON.
I SAW A SHUTTLE LEAVE THIS MORNING. I SUPPOSE THAT WAS THE LAST PEOPLE GOING.

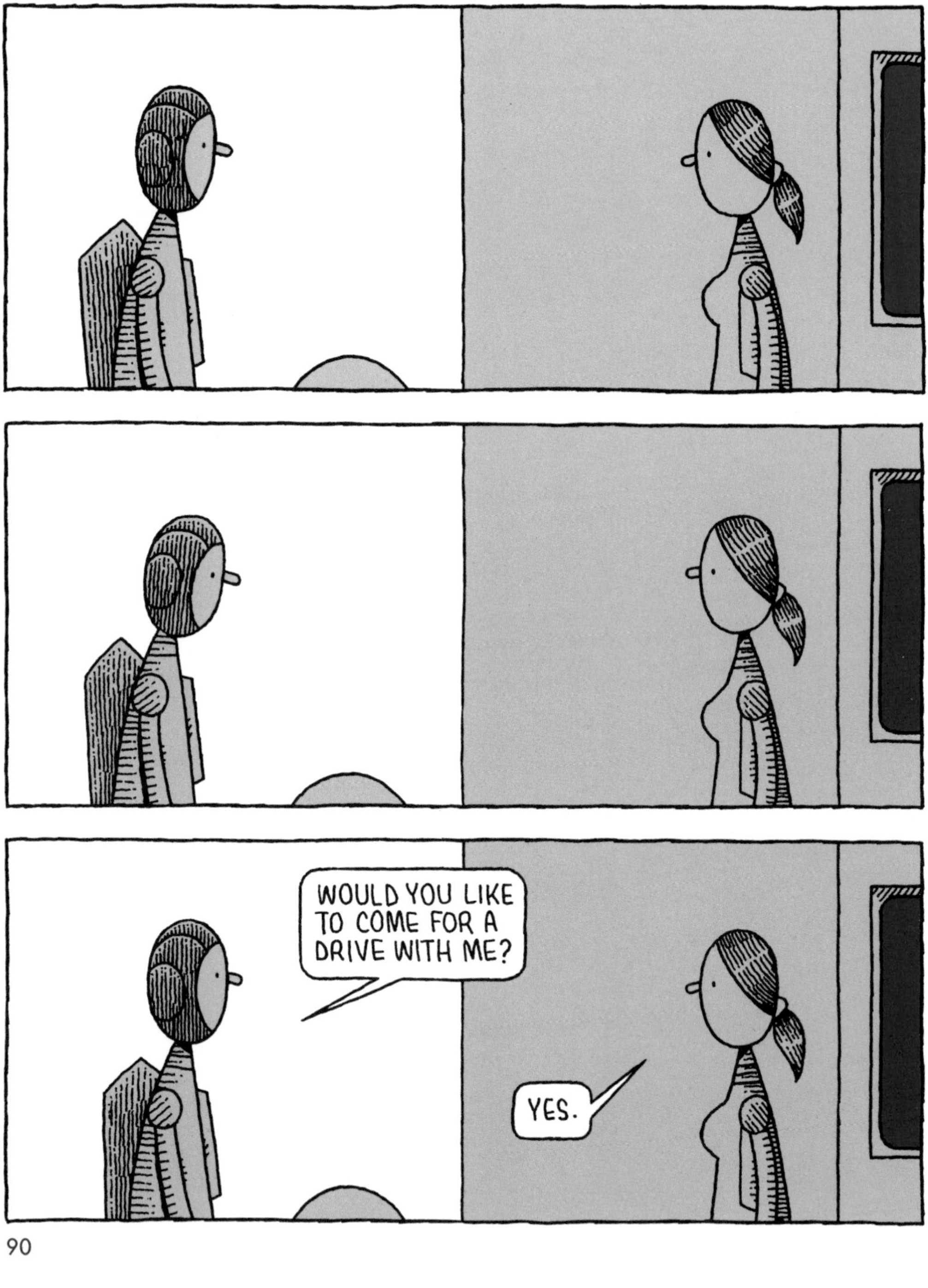
WOULD YOU LIKE TO COME FOR A DRIVE WITH ME?
YES.

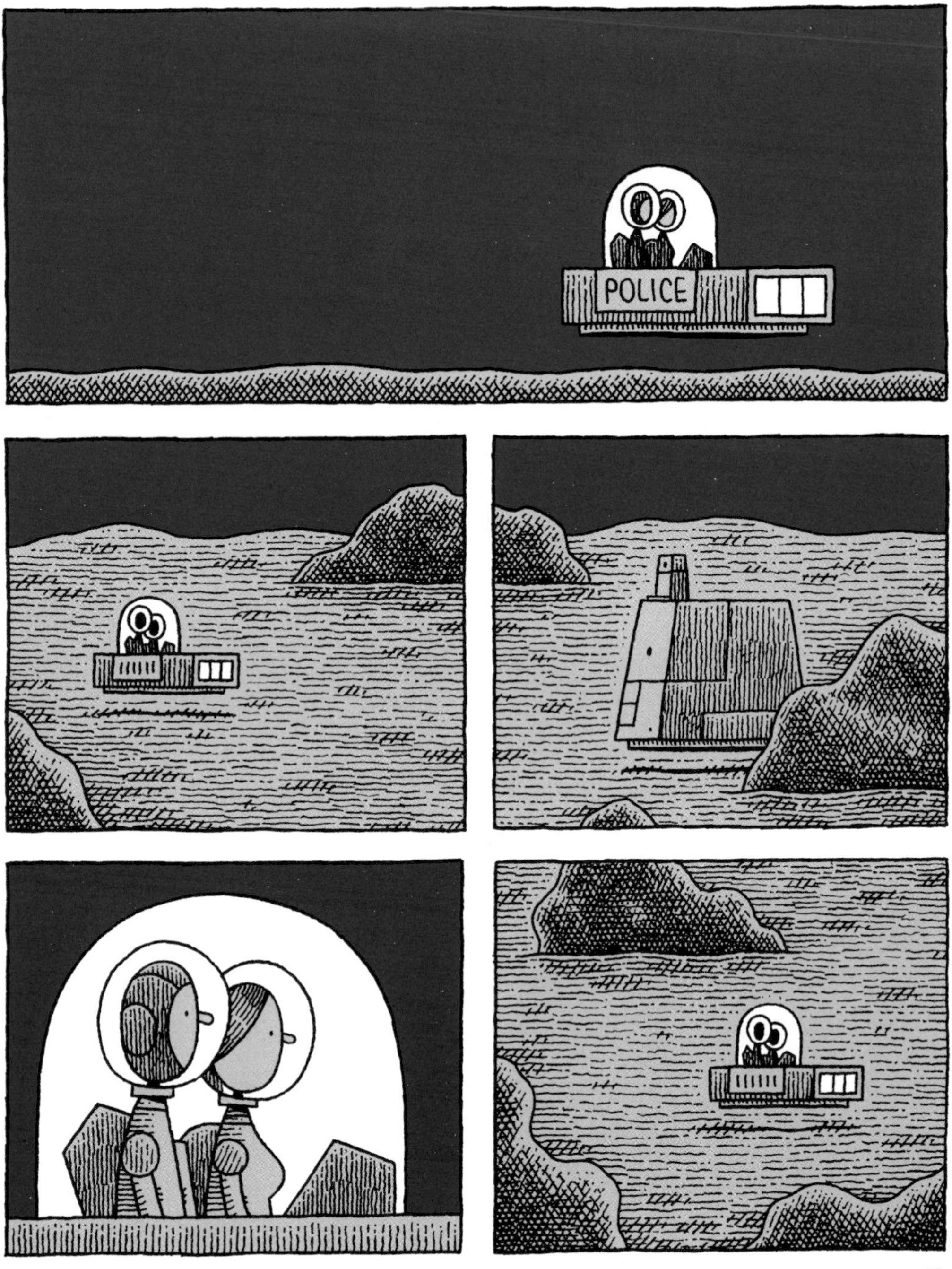
POLICE

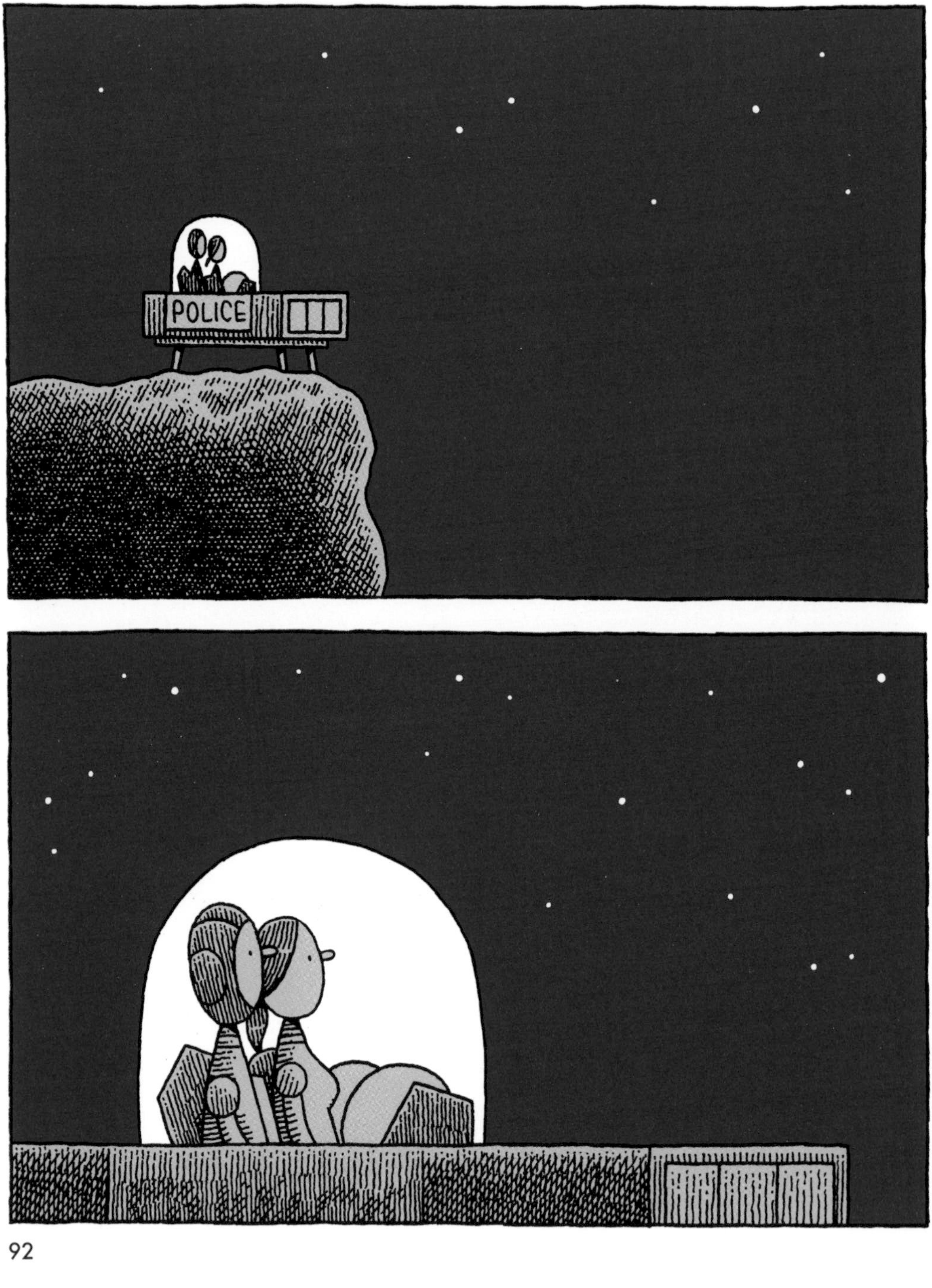
POLICE

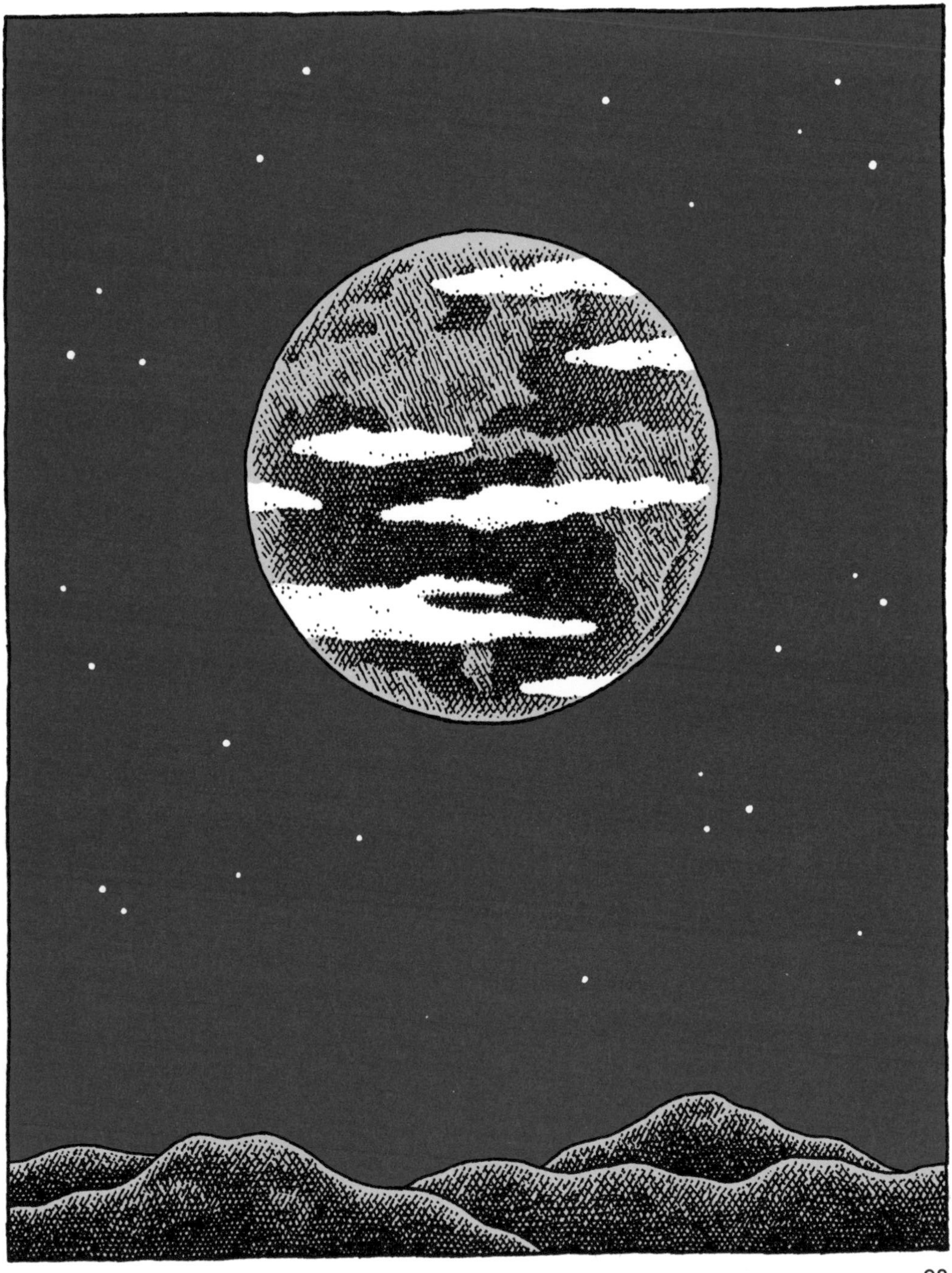

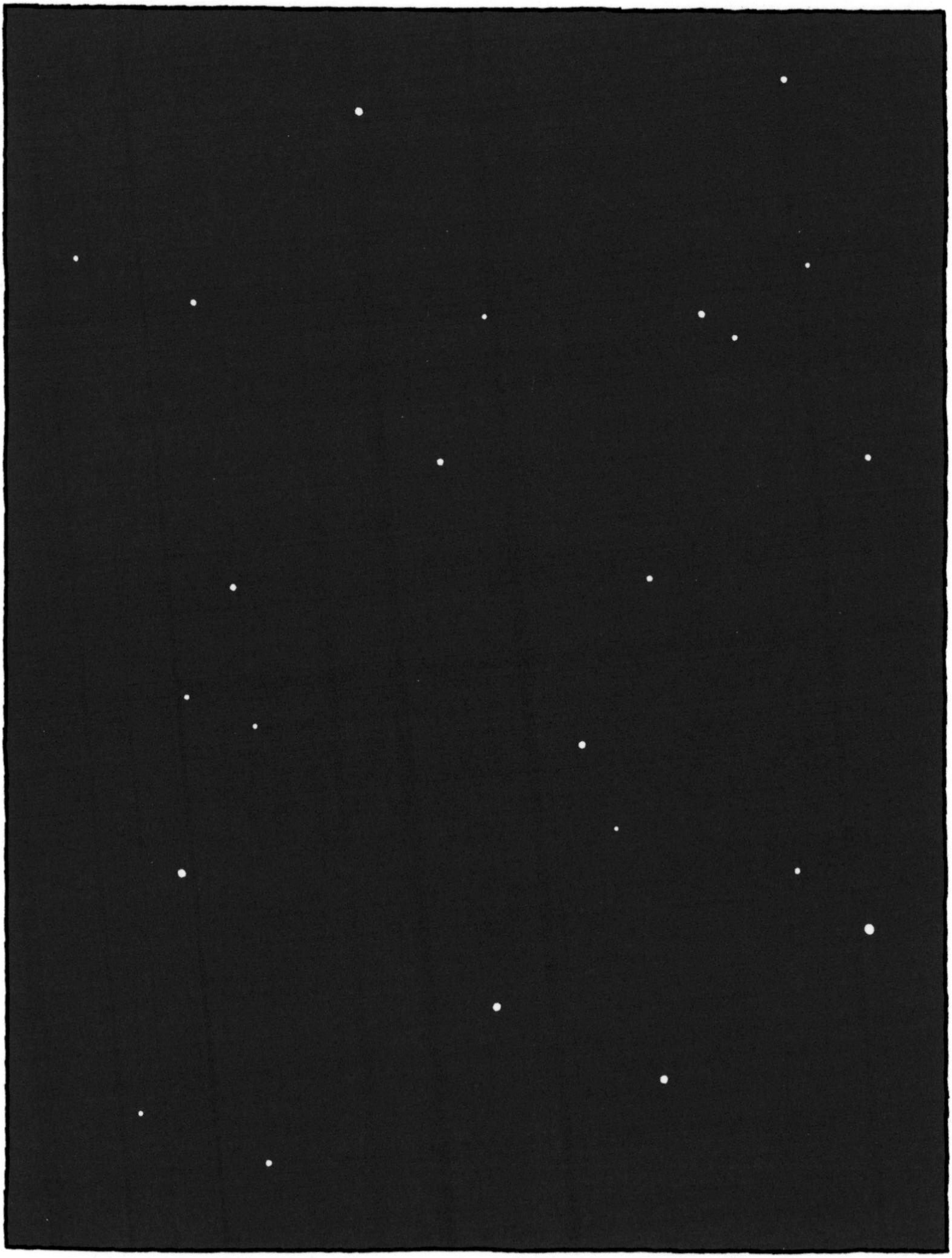

For Mum and Dad

Tom Gauld was born in 1976 and grew up in Aberdeenshire, Scotland. He is a cartoonist and illustrator and his work is regularly published in the *Guardian*, the *New York Times*, and *New Scientist*. His comic books, *Goliath* and *You're All Just Jealous of My Jetpack* are published by Drawn & Quarterly. He lives in London with his family.

Thank you to Jo Taylor, Billy Kiosoglou, Daphne Gauld, Iris Gauld, Peggy Burns, Tom Devlin, Tracy Hurren, Chris Oliveros, and Julia Pohl-Miranda.

TOMGAULD.COM | DRAWNANDQUARTERLY.COM

First edition: September 2016. Second printing: February 2017. Printed in China. 10 9 8 7 6 5 4 3 2

Library and Archives Canada Cataloguing in Publication: Gauld, Tom, author, artist. *Mooncop* / Tom Gauld. ISBN 978-1-77046-254-0 (hardback) 1. Comic books, strips, etc. I. Title. PN6737.G38M66 2016 741.5'9411 C2016-90 0983-1

Published in the USA by Drawn & Quarterly, a client publisher of Farrar, Straus and Giroux. Orders: 888.330.8477. Published in Canada by Drawn & Quarterly, a client publisher of Raincoast Books. Orders: 800.663.5714. Published in the United Kingdom by Drawn & Quarterly, a client publisher of Publishers Group UK. Orders: info@pguk.co.uk.